KAWOO OF ALASKA

Drawing of totem by Jerry Boyd

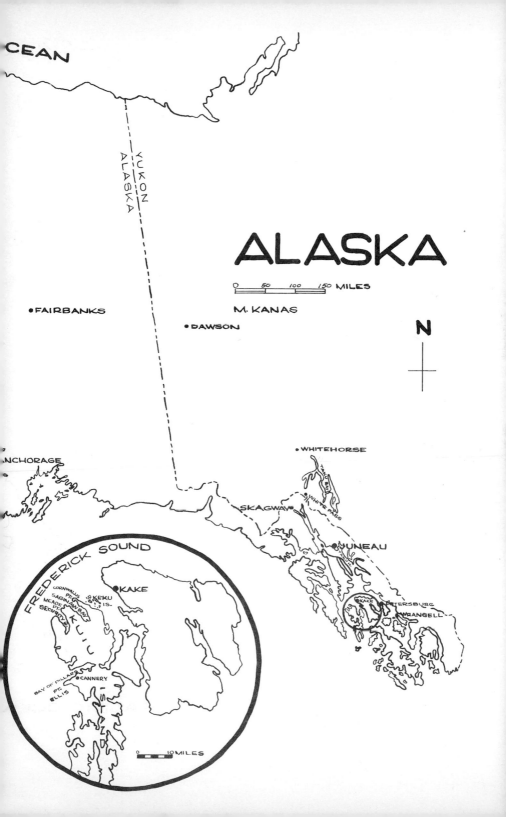

KAWOO
of
Alaska

GANO E. SENTER

SAGE BOOKS
DENVER

Sage Books are published by

Alan Swallow, 2679 South York Street, Denver 80210

FOREWORD

August 29, 1961. The Golden Wedding Reception was over. The old and young friends had departed, leaving us with the warmth of good wishes and a quiet time for retrospection.

It was difficult to realize that fifty years had passed since that sunny August day when my lovely blonde girl, still so lovely to me, and I had quietly eloped, to be followed by the prediction of family and friends that "the marriage would last not longer than six months."

With our daughters, Laurena Senter Evans and Alice Senter Maercklein, their husbands, and our grandchildren gathered around us, the oft-repeated plea from family members for the story of my early life had compelled me to promise them a record of those experiences.

Today, when shanghaiing is only a story depicted in a book or shown on a cinema screen, few people realize that it was a common practice in the early days of seafaring; that the cruelty the brutality of man's inhumanity to man was an actuality. Windjammers, which spawned those awful practices of shanghaiing, are familiar only to those who lived at the turn of the century.

I was shanghaied on a windjammer, finally escaping after three months before the mast and three months in chains, to fall into the hands of Tlingit Indians in Alaska, and escape from them after two and one-half years. Little did I realize, back in 1905, that I someday would be writing a book of my experiences and adventures. I had preferred, rather, to erase from my mind, the nightmarish spine tingling events that still return to me occasionally in my dreams, even though the later days of traveling in Alaska as shown in Part Two were interesting and enriching.

As I recalled my life with the Indians, however, I have often thought, "It is better to be a well-fed, well-treated slave than a starving, abused or dead sailor-castaway."

Through the opportunities of travel, which include two round the world trips in the past ten years and the privilege of seeing and studying many strange people and places, the happiness of years has eased the horrors of those early times. It is with gratitude to God, for his protection and guidance, that I dedicate this book to the loving family of the orphan boy,

Gano Senter

Denver, 1963

My Best Wishes to

From

"Kawoo"

Gano Senter

CONTENTS

PART I

PART II

PART ONE

SHANGHAIED

"The forecastle hands work like horses at sea and spend their wages like asses ashore. They are good at making and taking in sail, but they do not care for India and China voyages. They prefer to navigate between the dance halls of Cherry Street and the grog shops of Waterloo Road and Ratcliffe Highway."*

When the *Agenor* sailed from San Francisco in the spring of 1905, she had a crew of fifteen. Seven bearded Frenchmen had jumped ship and were seeking to get out of the country; among them were fugitives and convicts. The other eight members included a Portuguese, Irishman, Swede, German, Texas, Kansas farmer, my friend Harry, and myself.

On that fateful spring day, I, a husky fourteen-year-old, stood by a railing, looking longingly at a small freight steamship named the *St. Thomas.* Orphaned in 1904, my brother Clive had taken me from Denver to live with him in San Francisco. I was continuing my education in night school and working for the Eastman Kodak Company as an errand boy for three dollars a week. I had just made a bicycle delivery to a steamship company on the waterfront, when I was caught day dreaming by another delivery boy, Harry Cohn. After an excited discussion, we asked a stranger about the *St. Thomas* and were told she was a lumber packet, now loading and bound for San Diego just a few miles away. Since we obviously had a yen for the sea, he offered to

---

* Quote was recorded in the log book of the windjammer, *Agenor,* during one of the ship's last voyages.

help us get a berth on the *St. Thomas*. The owners were friends of his.

I informed Clive about our plans, and a few days later, after making our deliveries, Harry and I met with the stranger again, who reported that the *St. Thomas* had been moved down to the coal dock to fuel up for her trip. It would not be out of his way to escort us to the owner's office for an interview. We gleefully accepted, and the three of us walked over to a building on Jackson Street, where we entered through a door off the alley. Then, without warning, we were roughly shoved into a dimly lit room littered with straw mattresses and filthy blankets. The door swung shut and was bolted.

We waited, miserably but expectantly, for the promised interview. Darkness came, and with it three burly, battle-scarred men. Along with the mattresses and blankets, Harry and I were tossed into an express wagon. With a guard on each side of us, we were driven through alleys and back streets to an isolated dock on the waterfront. There we were thrown into a waiting gasoline launch and hustled out to the middle of the bay.

Suddenly, looming gigantically in front of us was the sinister black shape of a sailing vessel riding at anchor, with but two riding lights showing. The launch pulled up alongside and we heard the cry: "Cast me a line!" Whether from seasickness caused by the choppy ride out, or pure fright, I refused to climb the Jacob's ladder, and for my unwillingness was plainfully clipped on the jaw. "You'll either go up that ladder or down to the sharks . . . make up your mind!"

Such was our fortune that we boarded the ship *Agenor* instead of the *St. Thomas*.

PINK-CHEEKED BOY

The ship's deck looked deserted when we finally struggled aboard. Prodded by our guards, we stumbled over piles of rope, trying to follow a glimmer of light leading to the forecastle at the forward end of the ship. We staggered over bodies sprawled about the deck, twelve derelicts, whom Harry and I soon referred to as "the dirty dozen." Some were drunk, others drugged and seemingly dead, and still others just plain seasick. Harry and I, extremely sick, flopped onto a couple of bunks filled with straw mattresses called "donkey breakfasts" by the crew, to suffer our fate. The crew complete, the *Agenor* was underway. The waves rocked and heaved the ship as she was being towed outside the Golden Gate and out to sea.

At midnight the tugboat cut loose. "All hands on deck!" came the order, and bedlam followed. The Frenchmen, who spoke no English, could not understand the command; others were too drunk to hear it or too sick and beaten up to heed it. The mates waded in with belaying pins and marlin spikes, clubbing those nearest to hand, quickly rounding up a heap of lost and fear-stricken men who stood unsteadily. Another command was given to get aloft and unfurl the mainsail. English or no English, only the French able seamen now knew what to do. Still overcome by bewilderment, the rest stubbornly objected, but a smash to someone's chin and the threat of a gun forced all in the wake of the Frenchmen. Thus we labored up the rope ladders. An experienced seaman led a landlubber until every hand was aloft in the rigging.

13

I was ordered out to the end of the yardarm where I leaned over the spar on my stomach with my heels grooved in a half-inch cable. Fortunately, this was the correct procedure. When the ship leaned toward the starboard side, the end of the yardarm appeared to touch the water and the waves rushed up, breaking in phosphorus spray over me. Then, as the sails caught the wind, the ship righted itself and, from my wave-washed perch, I was lofted into the heavens again. Despite my being violently sick, I hung on, certain I was about to die and not really caring if I did. When the sails had been set, all hands were ordered below. I'll never know how I found myself at last safe on deck, a mop and swab in my hands, cleaning the results of my seasickness.

The first and second mates lined up the men and set about picking individual crews. The second mate, gun and lantern in hand, began selecting down the line. With a curse he reluctantly added me, a boy for a man's duties.

When the captain made his appearance at the forecastle, he faced a decidedly wretched and sullen group, not yet over the shock of waking up aboard a ship at sea, shanghaied. He looked us over, scowled, and then bellowed: "We have fifteen crew members on this vessel, provided one of you ain't dead!" He ordered a check of the crew and then muttered: "It's an ill omen to sail with a dead man aboard."

The second mate discovered the badly beaten and unconscious Texan and dragged him to his feet.

Someone whispered: "What in God's name happened to him?"

Overhearing, the second mate said: "He spoke when he should'a been listenin' so I worked him over. He hasn't learned to say 'sir' instead of 'huh,' see?" Dropping the lifeless body to the deck, the mate thundered: "Now listen you damned landlubbers, I am a 'sir,' the first mate is a 'sir,' and the captain is a 'sir,' so you learn now to say, 'Aye, aye, sir,' 'yes sir' and 'no sir,'

14

or you'll end up lookin' like this here bloke, understand, you land-lubbers?" Turning to the big Swede, Olaf, he demanded: "Understand?" Unfortunately, Olaf answered: "Uhuh." Whereupon, the mate grabbed a belaying pin, hit Olaf a resounding blow over the head and, hurling him across the deck, roared: "Say 'yes sir' you s.o.b."

The next morning all hands were called astern to the poop-deck where the captain and his officers waited with the ship's articles, which all sailors were required to sign. It was comparatively easy to sign up the Frenchmen who had jumped ship, and the Portuguese, although he was jabbering and shaking his fists. The Irishman protested in true Irish fashion, but, while one man held a gun on him, another slugged him, so he signed. The German kept insisting he was a mechanic, not a sailor. "You used to be a mechanic, you s . . . . ., you're a sailor now!"

I dreaded my turn with the Captain. He demanded to know what the hell I was doing aboard his ship. "This was a job for a rugged seaman, not a pink-cheeked schoolboy," he grumbled. "Was I a stowaway?" Well, he had a cure for stowaways. He signed them up for ten dollars a trip and unless he got work out of them, they didn't get fed. Harry received the same treatment!

The signing completed, the captain ended the episode by liberally praising the able French seamen, while damning and berating the remainder of the men, claiming they were not worth their salt. The captain and his officers considered their crew to be the scum of the Seven Seas.

We learned later, that 78 Jackson Street was the headquarters of the infamous "Shanghai Brown," who made a living shanghaiing a ship's crew at twenty dollars a head. His hirelings sought out men who were alone or strangers in town. It is no wonder the captain and the mates became known on the waterfront of

15

San Francisco as "as fine a gang as ever slit a throat or scuttled a ship."

The sails would be gathered in around the spars and tied about every four feet with a rope yarn to hold them in place against the wind. Our footing being only a half-inch wire cable, we would hang on spars until we could get into position to untie the sails. With equal speed of all hands, the entire sail would come down with a tremendous crash in mid-air and be picked up by the wind. Men on deck, on orders from the captain or mates, would pull on block and tackle ropes to put the sail in proper position with the wind. This was done on each mast and each set of sails.

Idle hands could not be numbered among the *Agenor* crew. If we weren't mending or trimming sails or splicing ropes, there were the perpetual jobs of painting the ship, and scrubbing the deck with a twenty-five pound holystone. And inescapable was the standing of watch at night.

One main responsibility of mine was to scrub down the ship's figurehead which was located at the bow. I'd be lowered down on a bosun's chair to a large spar, projecting forward from the stem of the ship, and still lower to the cutwater. With a bucket of soap suds I swabbed down the only lady aboard, while the ship would rear up on its hind heels and then come down on its bow, giving me a body wash in return.

On occasion we would depart from the normal run of duties. I recall one fishing spree when the mates rigged up heavy fishing lines with strips of salt horse and sowbelly for bait, and tossed the lines over the side. In a short time we had hooked a formidable nine-foot shark. After being hit in head with an iron belaying pin, the shark was pulled aboard where, aroused, he violently slapped the deck with his tail. The ship's carpenter, an evil-eyed, massive man of the sea, stepped up with a broad ax and aimed a powerful blow at the tail. Blood squirted in every direction as the shark floundered until he was dead. We had the task of skinning him, taking out the liver and rendering down some of the parts. The shark oil was used for dressing boots and oil-skin slickers.

We caught a second shark which was pulled out of the water and up to the ship's railing with a block and tackle. The ship's carpenter then tied a two-by-six wooden plank to the shark's tail, punched out both his eyes and lowered him back into the water. The shark was to die a lingering death by starvation, thereby satisfying the sadistic nature of the ship's officers. Yet their cruelty did not make the crew too unhappy. This was just one less shark to attack us if we were thrown overboard.

For the next two weeks we had shark steak at every meal. We didn't care if we ever hooked another one!

SHIPMATES

I would have thought that when men were thrown together under tyrannical officers, they would form friendships for each other out of pure sympathy. Such was not the case; here it was every man for himself. Surly, vicious, selfish men with more traits of savage animals than of man, made up the crew. Included were thieves and murderers. What reason to be friendly even if the opportunity could be had?

An attempt at humor often backfired. One Sunday morning, a crew member thought to shave and begged the cook for some hot water. His prize in hand, he whipped the pan full of green slime-water into a shaving lather. Not having a mirror, he was unable to see how ridiculous he looked with green suds hanging from his face. Several of us burst into a fit of laughter. Furiously he threw the water at us, charging across the foc'sle with his razor at the ready. Someone tripped him and he fell, cutting several bystanders on his way down. A free-for-all started, and the Sunday morning shave ended with many black eyes and bloody heads.

The ship's slopchest was open on the poopdeck. The slopchest was a commissary from which seaboots, slickers, socks, tobacco, and other articles could be purchased, against wages earned at the end of the voyage. Slim, 25, whose real name was Frank Smith, needed shoes, having lost one of his own when he was shanghaied. Astonished at the price of three dollars and a half for two-buckled plow shoes, he said: "Why, I get these kind back in Kansas for a dollar and a half."

The captain grinned slyly: "Aye, and you can get gold in Alaska and diamonds in Africa. You're a hellava long way from both of them, sailor. Either take 'em or get out!"

Seventy-five cent cotton shirts sold for two dollars. Sea boots and oil skins cost five times more aboard ship than on land. We realized that if we bought anything, we'd owe so much money when we did reach shore that we couldn't quit the ship. Most of us remained a dirty, bedraggled, half-dressed crew.

Since we were never allowed to talk to each other on deck, any discussions to be had always took place in the foc'sle. It was during these moments that the talk loosened up and wrathful vengeance was sworn against the ship's officers and the shanghaier, if they ever got back to San Francisco. Some suggested getting their vengeance now instead of waiting; most likely they would never see the waterfront again. Mutiny would have been brought about then and there, if someone in the group could navigate the ship into port. Threats to kill the captain were made, followed by fights over who would have the privilege when on land. Then the talk would switch to the individual shanghaiing experiences.

Big Boy, the barrel-chested Irishman, and his partner were sitting in a bar having a drink, when his partner went into the back alley and didn't return. Big Boy's search revealed a pair of legs sticking out of an ash can. His friend had been cruelly beaten. He reported to the bartender what had happened. The bartender laughed and offered to buy him a drink. Confused and angry, Big Boy gulped it down and that was the last he remembered until he awoke in the foc'sle of the *Agenor*, pockets empty and a enormous lump on his head. He was convinced that the liquor had contained knock-out drops.

As Big Boy sat thoughtfully rubbing his head, Olaf spoke up and told him it served him right for drinking, and launched into his own story. He had just been paid his month's salary of forty dollars earned in a lumber camp, and had come to town to have fun and find a woman. Well, he found one all right! She steered him to the back of a saloon where drinks were ordered through a window in the wall. "She hands me mine and leaves the room. I take a sip, hear something click underneath me and wow! A trap door opens and I'm sliding down a chute to the cellar. In a couple a minutes two big guys come in; one of them socks me on the head with a bottle. Next thing I know, I'm awake on this scow with no woman, no money and no future."

Portugee Toney was a weasel-eyed, dark-skinned sailor who had sailed the seven seas and had battle scars from all seven of them. Tony pulled on his mustache and in his broken English said: "You theenka you got troubles. My sheep just come from Japan to unload soma cargo and we have shore leeve. I'm a rich like hell, feefty dollar in my pocket. On the street a man aska for a match and a begin to talk. Pretty soon we go in a saloon to dreenk. We watcha fist fight with sailors, longshore-man anda bums. I tella my frend only foolish man fight with hands and get heemself all bloody. He say to me: 'How you fight?' So I show heem my sheef knife and I say nobody take knife away from me because I not get that a close to heem. I tell heem I can peen a man to the wall with this knife at thirty feet away and steek him against the wall like a bedbug with a peen through heem. I can cuta a throat without I getta my hands bloody. The man say: 'Let's take a walk.' So we walk to a saloon and dance hall with girls. I say let's go see girls. So we go in a side door into a leetle room and dreenk somethin' a beautiful girl brings us. I want to make heet with her, so I pulla out my beeg roll. Her eyes get beeger. She breeng an-other dreenk. My frend he leeva the room, and the girl she seet on my lap. Then it happen! The door behind me open, the door on a side open and three men coma in. One of them say, 'Huh, you steala my wife, huh?' I say, I no steala your wife. He say:

20

'You no foola me. You make a love to my woman. I gonna kill you.' Just as I reacha my knife to throw at heem, the man een back of me coma down on my head weeth a bottle. I wake up thees sheep and they keepa me lock up five days till we sail. I gotta two months pay comin' yet and the captain of my Spanish sheep, hees a gonna be mad because he theenk I desert his sheep."

As the victims recalled what had happened to them, tempers would rise and the vindictiveness against the officers was sworn anew. During one of these tirades, the cook had entered the foc'sle and we shut off the talk, knowing he was the captain's informer. He had heard enough.

The next morning, the captain and mates appeared on deck with guns. At noon we were piped back to the poopdeck where the riot act was read to us. He called it th Law of the Sea which meant he was lord and master of the ship and everybody on it. He reminded us that to strike a ship's officer would result in flogging, double irons, bread and water, and the logging of all our pay. If any of us was thinking of mutiny, there was a hell of a good yardarm we could swing from.

SHIP'S FARE

The captain's earlier threats to ration the food led me to belive it was really something special. Breakfast was a mixture of cornmeal and bran, three salt biscuits each, and black coffee. As each sailor filed by the cook in the galley, a ladleful of the mush was dumped into his tinplate. Nearby was a barrel of blackstrap sorghum, which was used instead of milk or cream on our "porridge." Lunch would invariably be salt pork and beans, hardtack and coffee. For dinner, curry and rice or cornbeef and beans. When the cornbeef ran out, which happened often, our fare was salt horse with beans or rice. Thursday we could always count on a mess of English plumduff, floating in an appalling sorghum dressing, which would lie for hours in our stomachs like a lead ball.

Food fanned many an argument. One rare calm day, our only opportunity to sit down and eat comfortably, a crew member reached across to Alphonse's pile of sea biscuits. Without a word, the Frenchman's knife came down on the foolish sailor's arm. "That's mine!" The sailor muttered that he didn't want the damned things; he only wanted to see how many maggots were in them.

Havoc reigned the time we were issued hardtack, green with mold. No one complained until the next day when the hardtack was served with dozens of fat, stubby, black-headed maggots wriggling out and about. The hardtack would walk away a half-inch at a time. The crew knocked out the maggots into a pile and took them to the cook, who in turn reported to the captain.

The captain paid a visit to the foc'sle. "Which one of you is complaining about fresh meat in your bread?" he roared. "You're damned lucky to get any! And the cook tells me you are unhappy about not getting enough potatoes." Holding up one finger and pointing it at the cook, he said: "Cookie, give these sailors all the potatoes they want." That evening we were served half a potato each; that finger was only half a finger.

THE STORM

When we asked what the ship's port-of-call was, we were told it was none of our damned business. About a week out, the quartermaster inadvertently said we were headed due north. He also remarked that we were lucky to have the lower hold full of rock salt for ballast because the barometer was low and a heavy sea was expected that night. Alaska was our destination; the rock salt was for packing 700,000 dog salmon.

The orders to take in sail and tighten down had been executed when the squall hit. I was on the midnight watch that awful night. The waves crashed over the ship from bow to stern and she was not responding to her helm as she should. Twice, I was almost washed overboard. My state of shock was apparent and my plight was reported to the second mate who tied me into the cat's-paw. "The captain would be wild if he lost a man, even if he was a 'pink-cheeked boy.'" The waves washed over me but my prayers were answered and I was still aboard when the nightmare ended.

Twelve barrels of oil had been lashed to the starboard and port sides of the ship on the main deck. To secure them, wooden cleats or chocks were nailed around the barrels with half-inch ropes. The ship heeled over to port at such an angle that it broke the lines on several of the barrels. In a matter of seconds, the four-hundred-pound drums of oil were shooting around the deck like cannonballs. As the fury of the gale increased, wind whistled and screamed through the shrouds. More barrels broke loose, and one slid forty feet across the deck, plunged through

24

the rail, and left a gaping six-foot hole. The next mountainous wave crashed down on the deck just as two barrels collided and burst. The skuppers were filled to overflowing, the crew on their hands and knees in a sea of oil and water.

A blast of wind hit the ship's sails ripping out a six-inch block and tackle. Falling from fifty feet, it crashed to the deck, striking one man on the head and shoulders and pinning another down. Several of the crew sprang to untangle them; but the first mate, cursing wildly, threw belaying pins at the would-be rescuers, ordering everyone back to trimming the sails. The two moaning men lay in agony many minutes before receiving attention. Safety of the ship came first, according to the Laws of the Sea and the mate.

I agreed with the captain that we were lucky to have the French seamen aboard. Without them, we might not have survived that stormy night. But since that experience, I have been convinced that oil and water can mix. They also mix with blood and seamen — the horror and screams of a man pinned to the railing by a barrel of oil, beyond help.

SAGINAW BAY

The weather for the next two weeks was favorable for sailing. Then came the cry of "Land-Ho!" and we entered Saginaw Bay, Alaska. Porpoises led the way, circling and playing alongside. At the mouth of the bay, we ran into a school of whales. Some were sleeping, their backs half out of the water looking like dangerous reefs. At the ship's approach, they spouted and with tremendous slaps of their tails, disappeared from sight.

After considerable maneuvering, we dropped anchor three miles off shore in the middle of the bay. For the first time in a month smiles wreathed the faces of the ship's officers. On the poopdeck, each of us received a cup of grog in celebration.

The captain and mates went ashore next morning to inspect the jungle of yellow cedar trees, which were suitable for replaceing the *Agenor's* rotten spars and yardarms. The captain had heeded reports from the Frenchman that the ship was in need of repair. A shore crew was chosen to do the lumberjacking and carpentry work. The rest of us were left to man the ship.

We had been in the bay for several weeks when a gasoline launch heaved into sight, from where I couldn't guess. The launch captain came aboard to make arrangements for the local Indian fishermen to supply us with salmon.* During the intervening time, the short crew floated the newly made spars and yardarms out to the ship to be lifted aboard and set in the proper

---

* At this time, Saginaw Bay was one of the many thousands of Alaskan bays inhabited solely by Indians.

places. With the rerigging of blocks and tackles and rigging up of new sails, the *Agenor's* gear was in perfect order.

The last job was scarcely finished when the launch captain and his engineer brought in the first of the fishing barges. Each barge was loaded with close to 40,000 salmon. With three-tined pitchforks, we soon found ourselves standing waist-deep in fish. We pitched the fish into a chute where they were gutted. A scoopful of rock salt was inserted into each, then the fish were pitched into another chute which delivered them to the lower hold, in the bowels of the ship. There the fish were stacked like cordwood, heads and tails alternating, and each layer covered with rocksalt until the entire hold was filled.

Loading took until the end of the salmon season. Meanwhile, the food and water became progressively poor. Scurvy broke out among the men, and I was one of the first to be unable to work. I was given the customary black pills which allegedly served as a cure-all for anything from a headache to syphilis. Syphilis, according to the captain, we would all have anyway after he got us to Japan. This threat was more frightening to me than the scurvy.

The launch captain, Olsen, had been in the foc'sle where I was quartered during the early stages of my suffering. From him I learned that some of our officers planned a water hunt to replenish the supply for the trip to Japan. He had found a map showing where a fresh water stream emptied into a bay. Olsen suggesed to the captain that he let me go along on the hunt.

The next day, four of us started down the coast. When we found the bay some forty miles from our ship, we also discovered an old deserted Russian saltry. By peeking through the holes in the walls, we could make out four halibut dories nestled one in the other. It was here that the water casks were filled.*

---

* The law required one gallon of water per day for each person aboard ship.

I had first thought of escaping the *Agenor* when I learned we were heading for Alaska. Now in this brief freedom, inhaling the scent of pine trees, I longed more than ever to escape the stench, sickness, and cruelty on the ship.

The sickness had grown worse and I was covered with open sores. Captain Olsen had shown concern and when he came aboard again, managed a visit to my bunk. "My God, kid!" he exclaimed. "You're going to die if something isn't done. I can't remember seeing a man in your shape before!" I told him about the black pills, three times a day. "Ah, those damned pills. Your captain is a pretty rough character, son. . . . I may be risking it, but I have to go for supplies one day soon and when I do, I'll think of something to get you off this deathtrap. I'll stow you away on my launch. Now, don't worry, I'll get word to you one way or another!"

I lived in hope for a week, then one of the shore crewmen came aboard and passed the word that the launch captain was leaving on the four o'clock tide the next morning. I made my plans.

ESCAPE

I confided in Slim, who had been kind to me during my illness, and who was just as determined to escape as I. When the ship's clock struck three bells, we started. My head pounding with fever, bare-footed, my only weapon a sheath-knife, I hung my shoes over my shoulder and crept out of the foc's'le. I crawled among the hawsers and ropes up to the poopdeck and the gangplank where the second mate was pacing back and forth. Crouching, I counted his steps and memorized them until I knew with my eyes shut when he would be at the port side of the ship.

The gangplank ran from the poopdeck to the ship's boat which was moored at the bottom. For about half an hour I counted steps and held my breath. Each time the mate turned on his heel, I'd gain a few feet. I finally reached the steps of the gangplank. On one of his turns, the second mate had come within three feet of me. He could have heard my heart pounding, had he listened sharply. I was glad he didn't, for I had made up my mind to use the knife if I got caught. I was scared, but any chance to be free was worth the risk.

I chose my time, watched him puff on his pipe, turn on his heel, and start back to the port side. The moment his back was turned, I was on the steps to the gangplank. Barely out of sight, I stopped and counted again, then made the last ten steps down the gangplank and into the boat.

Time stood still — Slim at last appeared. We cast off and clawed our way along the belly of the ship to the bow. We feathered the oars, which we used as paddles, and took off in the dead calm toward the shore at the end of the bay where Captain Olsen had camped.

Dawn was breaking as we arrived. The captain was preparing breakfast when I pulled open the flap of his tent. The startled man whirled around. "My God, what are you doing here?"

Instantly wary, I asked: "Well, aren't you leaving on the four o'clock fair tide?"

"Hell no! I'm not leaving for a week!"

"We got word on the ship that you were leaving," I cried out. "What shall we do?"

"Do? Go back," he commanded. "You'd better gives yourselves up. They'll kill you if they catch you."

I shouted that I'd rather be killed than go back.

"I don't care what you do, but get away from here. I don't want to be involved and I don't want any shooting around my camp."

Despite our shock and the shakiness of our situation, we set off toward the south, heading for the waterhole and the Russian saltry. I felt sure that we would find some signs of civilization around that area.

We saw the boats searching us out, but after a week of walking the beaches, keeping close under the foliage, we finally came to the bay. Across from where we stood was the saltry and the stream.

It was less than a mile across the bay, but to walk around it meant a forty-mile hike. I decided that one of us had to swim. Slim remarked that nobody swam in his part of the country, so I dove in. As I swam, my hopes soared. I had picked a target to swim toward and was making good progress when I was caught in a riptide. I became afraid that I would be pulled out to sea. Later, Slim told me that it was at this point I disappeared from his view. He had been panicstricken, not knowing

30

what to do. Helplessly but doggedly he waited, uncertain of my chances for survival.

Exerting every ounce of strength, I battled the riptide with eyes fixed on my target. It seemed to come no closer as the minutes dragged by; on the other hand, I didn't seem to be losing ground. I recited the Lord's Prayer in my mind. My lungs were near to bursting, but I kept praying and struggling. Then as if some giant monster had released his hold upon me, I found myself in calm water. I had turned on my back to rest, when a big push wave lifted me over the reef and onto the beach. My body had been gashed by the jagged rocks. I was half in, half out of the water, blue with cold. I realized later that the Japanese current and the chinook winds had made it possible for me to survive so long in the water. I was also thankful for my strong body, developed through athletic competition with my three older brothers.

I rubbed my shaking body with gravel to restore circulation, and then with bleeding feet, clambered over the rocks toward the saltry. The door was nailed shut, but with a large piece of driftwood I battered it down. Working my shoulders around the gunwales of the top dory, I managed to free it from inside the second boat. I attempted to turn the sixteen-foot-long boat sideways and ease it toward the ground. But it slipped off, fell four feet, and broke into a multitude of pieces.

With large rocks, I propped up one end of the gunwale of the next boat. Using my shoulder I lifted it six inches and pushed the rock down with my belly where it hit bottom in the third boat. I moved to the other end and repeated the process until I had built a foundation underneath each end. I pulled the boat up, turned it over on one side and slid it gently down to the ground.

Now came the task of getting the boat down to the water. I figured this out by gathering slick, slimy seaweed with which I built a path. I pushed the boat down this path and into the water where it promptly filled up like a sieve.

By this time my feet were bleeding profusely. I was discouraged and exhausted, but I pulled the boat out and drained it. I ripped my already ragged shirt into ribbons, and with chip and stone, I caulked the big wide seams with the pieces. It quickly swelled out in the water, appearing seaworthy.

A piece of driftwood served as an oar and I started back across the bay. Within a hundred yards of the far shore, the boat was shipping water heavily; then it sank. I stood up, amazed to find myself in four feet of water, beached on a mudflat. Slim, overjoyed, rushed to help me drag in the boat. He said he had seen buzzards circling above the water near the other shore and thought for sure they had gotten me. We used Slim's shirt for additional caulking and let the boat soak overnight. We had a boat, but didn't quite know what to do with it! By the sun, we could tell which way was south but didn't know if we were on an island.

The berries we had eaten on our way to the bay had all but cured my scurvy. We feasted again on the red and blue berries and inch-long salmon berries. The salmon berries reminded me of luscious raspberries and provided fluid as well as nourishment. We ate raw clams three times a day, occasionally building a fire and roasting the clams on sticks, which was a special delicacy. However, we were careful with fire for fear of revealing our camp to searchers.

We ran into a rainstorm at dusk while moving the boat up the bay. The skies turned completely black, and the peal of thunder was so loud that we frantically headed for shore and shelter. Drenched to the skin, we found entrance to a brush-covered cave revealed by a flash of lightning. As I cautiously entered, I smelled a peculiar odor. After I advanced six or eight feet, the odor became unbearable. I suddenly stared into a pair of brilliant eyes. I didn't move in time; a grunt preceded an ear-rending roar that echoed throughout the cave and then I was knocked flat. An enormous black bear stepped solidly on my stomach. Slim was given very nearly the same treatment as he and the bear met at the cave's opening. I don't know who was more frightened, Slim, me, or the bear.

It had been a two-day trip back to the site of the launch captain's camp. We came up the narrow strip of water, rowing into an inlet, from which we could see the ship riding at anchor. We hid our boat in the trees and cut across to the end of the bay to await darkness. Our plan was to approach Captain Olsen for help and something to eat. We waited in the long Alaskan twilight, close to the tent. The captain, about fifty years of age, a chunky and well-built fellow, was chopping wood and we could hear his wife repeatedly calling him to supper. Having had nothing to eat but clams and berries for nine days, our mouths watered for the food he did not seem to desire. We at last made our way to the tent, and I once again pulled open the flap.

Captain Olsen reached for his gun but took a second look at the dirty pair before him. "What the hell are you two doing here again? They're searching every island and bay around here and swear to take you dead or alive. It's a smart thing I didn't have you aboard when I went up to Juneau for supplies last week because your captain searched every inch of my launch."

We recounted all that had happened to us and he called us a couple of stupid fools. "Going south around an island — you'd get nowhere that way."

His wife protected us from a further scathing and suggested he give us "poor boys something to eat before they starved." The captain handed each of us a plate of very fine pork and beans and bread. In spite of his cautioning, we ate until we could eat no more and then became violently ill, only to lose the whole wonderful meal.

He didn't want us around his camp because another search for us was to begin in the morning.

"I'm going to give you fellows another chance to get out. I'll draw you a map. That damned old boat you've described wouldn't carry you another mile but you can have my little dinghy. It will at least take you to where you're going, if you do as I tell you," he said hopefully.

"This number one island out here is the one you stay away from," he warned us, while his finger began to circle the map. "That is known as Kupreanof Island, and the unfriendly tribe of Kake Indians lives there. They are considered the terror of Southeastern Alaska. White hunters and prospectors would rather be blown out to sea and perish, than try to get shelter with those Indians. Stay away from that island and go to number two island."

The captain instructed us how to get past the ship, keeping close to the shore, and then out to sea around the point where we would find a sandy beach. "Pull up there and remain until daylight," he emphasized, "then row swiftly and you'll make this number two island before the ship's officers are out looking for you. On number two island remain out of sight until just before dark and then row hard again to this number three island. Stay there all night and the fourth day you'll make this island here," and he pointed specifically. "From here you can make Petersburg, which is the big fishing village. You'll have enough grub to carry you through!" He was referring to the box of groceries that his wife had fixed up for us. "Good luck and get out of my sight!"

We paddled quietly along the shore and out to rough water where we thought we were out of the bay. The small boat rolled and tossed in the black night. When we fancied we had rounded the point, I got up to the bow and touched bottom; it was rocky. We hadn't found the sandy beach. We decided to pull the boat

34

up in the rocks and curled under a tree to sleep, not realizing it was high tide.

The sun was bright when we woke. We had overslept. The tide had gone out and the boat was hung up by the bow, high and dry, and all the food and utensils were gone. In desperation, we ran back into the woods, ate all the berries we could, dug clams at the shore line and set off on foot to check our position.

We had not rounded the point! Returning to the boat, we pushed off from the rocky beach and from under the high cliffs jutting out on one side of the island. As we made our way to number two island, we were caught in cross currents and swept back around the point in full view of the ship which was anchored about six miles away. While we were straining to get back to shore, we heard the putt-putt of a gasoline engine, and within a few minutes the launch came in view. Heading straight for us was the captain, second mate and the ship's carpenter, all armed with guns.

Although we pulled for dear life, we soon heard the command to cease rowing. I yelled, "Don't do it, Slim. Pull hard to shore. We can throw boulders down on them from the cliffs." But we were still in the rough water and could make no headway.

The captain turned the launch directly into our dinghy, and overboard we went. I felt a boathook run down my neck and body. Someone grabbed me by the seat of the pants and hauled me up, handcuffing me as I came over the side. Next came the leg-irons and I was tossed down into the engine pit. Slim joined me and back to the *Agenor* we went where we were unceremoniously dropped into a barge-load of fish. Cursing us, the second mate took off our leg-irons and told us to unload those fish. He also remarked that since we had been living off the fat of the land, we wouldn't be in need of any food.

We pitched fish all night and, in the morning, were given a breakfast of blackstrap sorghum and bran mush. Then we were

35

taken below and locked up in the chain locker with a thirty-day bread and water order against us.

It was an unbearable and tortuous nightmare that I somehow and unbelievably survived. The eyes of the rats gleamed in the black hole; their teeth nipped constantly at our bodies. I learned, here, the meaning of the word bilge rat, for I had become one of them. They screeched, fought and scrambled all over us. The food was sent down in a bucket and we would eat what we could of it, and let the rats fight for the rest.

At the end of three weeks we saw a beautiful daylight. More of the men had come down with scurvy, and our hands were needed. "Did you have enough?" the mate asked. We assured him that we were ready to do our jobs.

Back in the hold full of rock salt, the sores on my feet began to bleed again. I had been forced to remove my shoes because of the massive swelling, and the salt ate into my cuts until the intense pain was nauseating. When I next saw the mate, he informed me I would have to return at night to the locker so I couldn't escape again. I complained to him about my feet and he accused me of being a bad influence on the crew. However, I was allowed to return to my bunk and the black pills, but my condition continued to get worse. My body was covered with gaping sores.

One day I felt a jostling of the ship, then heard strange voices. I hobbled across the deck, peeked out, and saw the steamer *Alki* tied up alongside.

The steamship was loading us with provisions for the voyage to Japan. I stared into the face of a white-coated waiter from the *Alki* and he jumped back in horror, as though he had seen a ghost or a leper. He asked what in God's name was the matter with me and why wasn't I in the hospital. I said the only hospital we had was Davey Jones' Locker. He was shocked that

36

we did not carry a doctor on board, but, then, he had never been aboard a windjammer before. Indeed, he was accustomed to the pampered life of a steamer sailor.

He volunteered to help me. "I'll stow you away on the *Alki* if I can. Your captain and mates are back on the poopdeck drinking like fish from the kegs of rum we just put aboard. You stand fast in the doorway and I'll go back and watch your officers. When the time is right I'll signal and you make a run for the rail." Then he asked if I could walk. I nodded.

The signal came in about ten minutes and I struggled up and over the four-foot rail, jumped three feet across to the *Alki*, and fell down under the rail and out of sight. I lay still until the waiter motioned me to run. He led me down between decks, through four or five passages, into a rope locker. I crawled into a large coil of two-inch hawser with the customary hole in the center. He put a couple of sacks of rope over my head and went out, locking the door.

Hot water was dripping down my neck and into my sores. I figured I was under the donkey engine and it was leaking. It seemed an eternity that I huddled in this cramped position, wondering and waiting. Then came pounding on the door and orders to open up. I heard the voices of my captain and his mates. The door was soon opened and they started the search with pistols in hand. For a brief moment, I thought they wouldn't find me, but a mate picked up a sack of rope which had covered my head, pushed my coil of hawser over and kicked in the top of it. I backed out the other end. A pair of handcuffs, the twister kind, were clamped on my wrists, and I was smashed on the jaw. A gangplank stretched between the *Alki* to the *Agenor*, across which I was dragged and kicked to the deck below while the steamer crew watched in dismay and protested loudly.

The *Agenor* captain, with a wave of his pistol, shouted back

37

that he was exercising his rights under the Search and Seizure Act for maritime deserters and that anyone who interfered would be shot.

The ships were untied and the signal was given to cast off. Away went the steamer and with it another chance to leave this desolate ship.

I was clapped in double irons and put back in the black hole, but this time I was chained to the rudder post, having just enough room to sit up. In rough weather, the rudder would swing and my arms were pulled starboard to port. And still there remained the rats and the stench of the bilge water, and the ever-infested food. I didn't think I'd make it this time.

I considered the events of this last near escape. I could have made a clean getaway, had the rest of the crew not had the same idea. The *Agenor* officers, even in their drunken state, could not help but see them abandoning ship. The steamer captain had to yield to the marine right of search. On boarding the *Alki*, they rounded everyone up, counted them, then looked for me in my bunk.

My sentence was for thirty days. After two weeks the mate came down to unlock my handcuffs and say: "Now you need some exercise. Here's a hammer and chisel. Chip the rust off the anchor chain, forty feet every day." Each link was about six-inches long. The mate checked my work every few days. In a week's time he said: "We need you up on deck. More men are trying to die on us. But you'll still be locked in here at night." So I went back to work on the fish gang.

HOPE

The *Agenor* was about to set sail. The salmon fishing was nearly over. I had one hour of liberty after work for supper, and then someone would yell "Callaboose" and I'd be taken below and locked up. During this break one night, a group of Indians paddled out to the ship in half a dozen canoes and came aboard. The Indians traded venison and bear meat, and also, a number of fresh, big beautiful deer for soap, matches, tobacco and whiskey.

One canoe had been left on a long line and had drifted up to the forward end of the *Agenor*, where I spotted it. Without hesitating, I tied a heaving-line fast and slid down into the canoe. Harry Cohn saw what I was up to and on the spot decided to leave with me. We hugged in close to the ship, pushing back to the stern where the ship's boat was tied. Scrambling from the canoe into the boat, we edged our way along the bow and stroking hard, headed for shore. Half an hour later we pulled up on the beach where we were immediately surrounded by Indians.

Using pidgin English, I explained to them that we were escaping and needed a place to hide. We were put in a big canoe with squaws, kids and dogs. We sailed all night, beaching in the early morning at the Indian home camp. I had been in such a cramped position that I could scarcely move. The Indians looked at me suspiciously, for they were very much afraid of cripples or crazy people. I assured them the best I could that I was strong in spite of my sores, and then they escorted Harry and me into the camp.

These Indians were helping to supply the salmon for the *Agenor*. They told me that the captain of our ship was a bad man and that he had cheated them on the fish count. They also said that the steamer from the cannery was coming to take them and their empty barges back to their summer fishing home called Quatahein, meaning "plenty of rain," or, in English, Point Ellis.

They fed us a plateful of seaweed, which was as salty as brine, a handful of hemlock bark, and a large spoonful of herring eggs. I was invited to help myself to some venison from the two hind-quarters that hung roasting over the fire. We had a combination of foods the like of which I had never imagined before.

My companion, Harry, turned up his nose at the Indian food. While I, with ravenous appetite, considered it a banquet, Harry would repeatedly complain that he didn't like this and couldn't eat that. Something instinctively told me he was doing the wrong thing. The Indians were not pleased with his manners and gazed at him with disdain and many frowns.

We assumed the search for us was started, although we hoped the officers were tired of that game. Harry and I agreed that if we saw them coming we would take to the woods. On the fourth day with the Indians, we saw a boat approaching and we fled into the timber. I knew that the woods were full of wild animals but I'd take my chances with them or the Indians, rather than with the ship's officers again. I took off over a mountain, planning to circle around and be back by nightfall. Harry worried about the dangers of the forest and went only a short distance, to wait near the trees.

The smoke we had detected had come from the tug that the Indians were expecting. Ready to leave, the Indians blew the tug whistle, signalled, and yelled for us. Harry heard them and went aboard without me.

I returned just before dark and thought I had missed the campsite, but I poked out plenty of evidence to the contrary.

Dogs had left scraps of dried fish and fins, which I ate promptly. Then I waited for someone to return for me. I waited in vain and for a week I prowled the beach. I had been with the Indians just long enough to learn some tricks for combatting the wilds. At low tide I would go to the rocks and, with my knife, pry off a type of barnacle sea louse, which is not poisonous and very nourishing. I found the seaweed that I knew the Indians liked and discovered that hemlock bark could be filling.

One day I would go north on the island in search of food, and the next day head south, but I always returned to my home base at night. From the south side of the trees, I carried armfuls of dry moss and piled it up to make a nest, into which I crawled at night and slept in fair comfort. In the morning I'd dig clams for breakfast and then start berry hunting. Only the tough, dry berries could I find now.

I waited patiently and with great apprehension for someone to come, and as time passed, I began to wonder. Winter was ahead. Would I be able to survive?

HORROR ISLAND

As the nights grew colder and the days shorter, my entire thoughts were filled with misgivings. I would remember the stories I had heard of the savage Kake Indians and their hatred of white men. I sensed that it was not the Kakes that had brought me to this campground because they had not shown cruelty. What would be my fate if I were found by the Kakes? I also recalled Captain Olsen's warning, which did not make me feel any better.

My panic increased to the point that I didn't doubt my eventual death, one way or another. The food supply was inadequate and I had nightmares about being left alone to freeze or starve. I was afraid to drift too far off from camp for fear of someone coming and missing me. As I lay in my moss nest listening to the threatening cries of wolves, I fancied they were as hungry as I and soon would come to eat me.

However, the urge to live forced me to forage. One day I smelled the strong, pungent odor of the wild deer and I eagerly started to search. Then I found the real source of the odor. Hanging on a tree were two sets of scent bags or musk from the sex glands of a buck deer. I remembered now the Indians going to examine their deadfall pits. I found such a pit which was about five-feet deep and hooked the scent bags, one on each side, then covered the pit well with brush. At sundown I returned and beheld my victim, a fawn deer, his large brown eyes pleading.

Because my hunger was stronger than my pity, I cut his throat. I had no matches and had to resort to eating it raw. I licked the warm blood off my hand and it tasted good; so I skinned the meat out partially and took a bite, chewed, swallowed and up it came.

I thought of the Colorado man-eater, named Packer, accused of eating five of his companions while he was acting as their guide in the early gold-rush days of 1873. And I couldn't eat a deer? By cutting the meat in very small pieces I was able to swallow it with the aid of a dash of salt water. It stayed down.

As nightfall approached, the wolves picked up the scent of my fresh kill and moved in closer. I spent an alarming night protecting that carcass, and almost wished I didn't have such a prize. One thing was sure, I did not intend to share it with a wolf. At down, I dragged my fawn to the water's edge and placed a big rock on it, then waited for the high water to cover it. I had no more worry from the wolves except for their continuous howling at night. My main problem was that I could only get meat to eat when the tide was out.

I had lost all track of time, but I would guess about the ninth day of my lonely abandonment, I spotted a tiny speck on the horizon. It materialized into a canoe with a sail, carrying an Indian and his squaw. I was so terrified of being captured by the Kake Indians that I fled up the mountainside and through the jungle. From a vantage point, I watched the couple pull up alongside my fawn, which was exposed, and stare in astonishment. On the beach were my footprints which they tracked immediately. In about an hour, they came directly on me, the Indian carrying a rifle, and the squaw a long spear. A torn, ragged and very scared young boy sat frozen to the spot. The man beckoned to me to stand up and head down the mountain to his canoe. He loaded me with the fawn into the canoe, paddled out and set sail. That evening we pulled up on another island and took shelter in a trapper's old lean-to.

A fire was built and a pot of seaweed was cooked, along with

43

a pot of Indian tea made from an herb called Yonnate. My venison was roasted to a golden brown. How I did enjoy that feast. But more important, I relaxed in the company of these Indians.

We beached the next day at Quatahein, the same village that had been mentioned by the Indians who had supplied the salmon. I noted probably twenty or thirty shake houses, twenty or so boats, a few barges, and so many dogs I couldn't count them.

My captor left his squaw to guard me while he went into the tiny village. About fifty Indians came down to look at me, then gestured for me to get out of the canoe. Soon my captor appeared with a short, stocky, prosperous-looking Indian. He regarded me while the other talked enthusiastically. The stocky one shook his head in the negative, at which point my captor dragged out the carcass, and the stocky Indian's face lit up. I heard the word "Killasnoo" frequently used and I thought it meant that they were going to kill me. I heard many more bewildering words which sounded ominous to me, but which I later learned were simply the names of the Indian tribes or other towns.

Quite abruptly I was led up to a large house. The stocky one entered, then returned with twenty fiery-red blankets and gave them to my captor. Without a backward glance, my captor and his squaw left the house and embarked in their canoe. There was no doubt in my mind; I had been literally sold into slavery.

In time I found out that the recognized medium of exchange in this particular tribe of Indians was the blanket.

Within a year or so I knew enough of the language to learn that another tribe had considered dickering for my person. I was known to be on the island, but fear kept most of the Indians away. However, it did not take me a year to discover that I was in the hands of the dreaded Indians from Kake.

CAPTIVE

My purchaser was a member of the Kake Tribe of the Tlingit Indians. As I absorbed their unwritten language, my respect for these Indians grew in many ways. My new owner, a man of about 45 years, occupied a high rank in the tribal clan and councils, which was to my later advantage. His squaw was fat, ugly and nearly six-feet tall, but she had a good heart and liked me.

Since my new owner had paid such a high price for me, he was anxious to protect me from the captain of the *Agenor*, who, I made him realize, was a dangerous man and was looking for me. There were boards over the rafters in his house and I was deposited in this little loft to sleep or hide whenever a strange ship was sighted off the coast. Word ultimately turned up, however, that the *Agenor* had sailed from Saginaw Bay. I took comfort in that news, despite my present situation.

The cannery closed and the hunting and fishing season was ended, when Harry reappeared. Many of the Indians were leaving the village daily for their various winter headquarters. Harry's captors were going to Kupreanof and the town of Kake, where they would hold the winter potlatch.* My destination was still unknown to me.

Meanwhile, my owner and I made many excursions into the forest to cut cedar timber for the boat that would take us out to sea. I marveled at his amazing skill in the two month period of time that it took him to construct a twenty-eight foot sailing boat.

---

* Potlach is a ceremonial festival where gifts are distributed by a chieftain or man of means in a show of wealth and importance.

One piece of a complete tree which was bent in the groin in the shape of a right angle, formed the stem of the boat. Then a twenty-four foot keel cut of timbers was attached onto the stem piece. No nails, bolts or reinforcements were necessary as dowel pins were used. He launched the boat during a gale and displayed magnificent seamanship as he fought the head wind and reefs on both sides. After three days, we sailed into the village of Kake where eight hundred Indians were assembling for the winter.

We were met at the beach by numerous Indians who came to see the second of the two captured white boys. I asked about Harry, but no one seemed to know anything about him. That same day I traced down the Indians Harry had left with from Quatahein. They evasively informed me that Harry had been captured by the Cushtaka. Who or what was the Cushtaka? Eventually, I was told that on the journey to Kupreanof, Harry had convulsed, foaming at the mouth and rolling his eyes wildly. Since the Indians were terrified of "crazy" people, he was thrown overboard where he had been "captured" by Cushtaka, the evil merman who was half otter, half man. I was told that Cushtaka took possession of all people who were lost at sea. This was my first introduction into the many mystic spirits, totems and myths of the Kake Tribe. The complexities of the Indian's beliefs were very confusing to a boy of my age.

My life with the Indians revolved around working, eating and sleeping, and, aside from my acceptance into the tribe, I took little notice of their mythological beliefs and customs. A number of the Tlingit beliefs were recorded however, by Dr. Hartley B. Alexander a few years after my stay with the Kake people.*

---

* Hartley Burr Alexander, *The Mythology of All Races*, Vol. X, North America, Copyright 1916 Marshall Jones Co., printed in the U. S. by Plimpton Press, Norwood, Mass.

INITIATION

Shortly after my arrival at Kake, I was taken to a building in the village and into a large room where squaws were seated on benches around all four walls. A fire burned in the center; a whole deer was roasting on the spit. I was pushed forward and told to help myself to a bowlful of food evidently prepared especially for me.

Suddenly, drums began to beat outside, and just as joltingly, the room began to echo with a high-pitched keening of women's voices, an ear-rending sound which sent shivers through me. The squaws stared at me blankly; then, as if directed by some unseen hand, they started to beat in rhythm upon sticks. The last bit of food stuck in my throat as I, with foreboding, eased toward the doorway.

Cautiously peeking out, I beheld an awesome sight. A rite of some kind was taking place on the beach, where nearly a hundred Indians were gathered, all dressed in full ceremonial regalia. Each modeled grotesque, but spellbinding, wooden animal masks which, to the Indians, represented supernatural beings. The masks were hand-carved and intricately painted. Later knowledge revealed that each mask symbolized a particular mythical character. The chiefs wore elaborate war bonnets stuffed with swansdown. Thrust through the tops of the bonnets were walrus whiskers. The entire group was armed with great, long spears.

They concluded the mysterious pow-wow, and, to the accompaniment of the booming drums and the squaw chorus behind me, headed straight for where I stood. I hurried back to the fire, crouching there to wait my annihilation.

47

In single file, the Indians entered the room circling the fire in a weird earth-thumping dance, until at last they closely surrounded me. Now that the drums were inside, the noise was deafening. The dancers became more frenzied as they shouted, "Huggee, Huggee!"* I stiffened when a spear whistled past my head and imbedded itself in the solid wall. At the same moment, an Indian leaped over the roasting deer, landing on his feet in front of me. He shook his great bonnet several times and the room filled with a storm of swansdown. After many leaps, the air was so thick with down I could hardly breathe. Occasionally an Indian would seem to faint. A medicine man would rush up, brush the soles of his feet with a raven feather, and the fellow then leaped up to join the race again. The fallen ones were supposedly possessed by a spirit. In the spirit world of the Tlingit Indians, the Raven, despite adversity, is a magician who never loses his great power or strength.**

The ceremony continued for hours, or so it seemed, with the spears whistling around my head and the swansdown whirling like a Colorado blizzard. All at once, the uproar and movement terminated.

The chiefs now formed in a group and the rest assembled around the fire. Speeches were made, songs sung, and poems recited by the chiefs and the older members of the tribe. Following each recitation, the performer would tear a blanket in half: one half of the blanket was placed at my feet and the other half in front of an Indian, until there were blanket halves in front of everyone.

My owner then appeared from behind a mask to claim me, marking the end of the celebration. It was finally made clear to me that this was my initiation and adoption into the tribe. I wasn't going to be executed after all!

---

* Jump, jump.
** Hartley Burr Alexander.

Gano Senter in 1905, age 14.

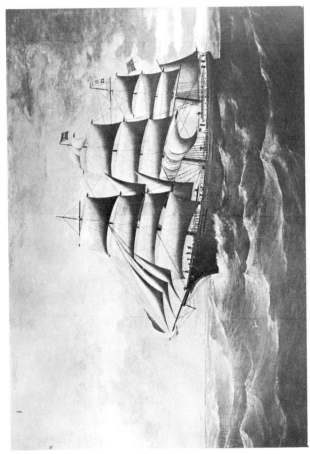

The *Agenor* was launched in April, 1870 in Boston. She was 202 feet by 39.9 by 24.2 feet and registered 1414 tons. Early in her career the *Agenor* made several transatlantic voyages. She also took coal to the West Coast of South America, then proceeded to San Francisco with grain for Europe. Thereafter, she sailed between Atlantic ports and those of the North Pacific Coast and the Far East. She was operated in the export lumber trade out of Puget Sound, at which time she was sold to parties in San Francisco in 1905 who sent her to Alaska. *Photos courtesy The Peabody Museum of Salem.*

Kake Indians wearing ceremonial costumes.

Results of an Alaska bear hunt.

Alaskan Indian costumes.

The totem whale tooth killer whale presented to Mr. and Mrs. Senter at Kake ceremonial, May, 1964.

PHOTOS OF THE RETURN
OF KAWOO TAKEN
BY LAURENA (MRS. GANO E.) SENTER

Point Ellis, Alaska.

The Raven, Kake, Alaska.

Kawoo with Kake Indian friends.

Gano and Laurena Senter in Kake Church.

Kake, Alaska, in May, 1964.

Deadman's Island, Alaska.

Alaskan mountains and glaciers.

57

Keku Islands, Alaska.

Roy Peratrovitch and Kawoo.

Kuiu Islands, Alaska.

Laurena and Gano Senter on trip to Kake.

Susie, Martha, Danny, Serg. Tom, with Gano Senter, February 15, 1964.

The famous Senter Christmas Tree.

KAWOO KETCHTOOYACK

I was called Kawoo, which was the name of the fuzzy growth on the belly of a salmon. The fuzz is visible just before the salmon goes up the river to spawn and die. My long-blond hair probably reminded the Indians of the salmon growth. Besides, they didn't expect me to live but a brief existence.

I was also given my owner's family name of Ketchtooyack. Kawoo Ketchtooyack—and my owner was now my father or my "Ish." I was accepted as a member of the tribe, and with special privileges. I was no longer a slave. I could go anywhere, on anyone's land. Ish indeed had power, or at least great influence, because Indians never trespassed on another tribe's hunting or fishing grounds. Trespassing was known to hold certain death, for why would a man go on another's property for any reason other than robbery? My Ish assured the tribe that I was unable to bring evil spirits and that I had nothing to do with witchcraft. I was no kin, he said, to the six-foot-six giant white trapper, who could walk in the snow with one foot pointing in one direction and the other in the opposite direction. The Indians ran that trapper with the swivel hip socket off the island.

I can still see father swell with joy and pride when my Indian mother or Eclaw would tell me to call him to dinner. I would approach him among a group of Indians and shout, "Ish-auk-ta-et-ke-ka," which meant, "father, come home to eat." This stern looking and strict man with his little mustache would smile and bow and we'd walk back to our home. I was free labor of course, though not a slave, but this man of royal prestige was honored to have this white boy for a son. Eclaw made good Indian clothes for me: a long-tailed buckskin shirt, a furlined coat and mukluks (sealskin boots).

I became accustomed to sleeping in a sixteen by sixteen room that was often occupied by my father's fishing crew and their families or by visiting relatives.* The house was built of half-inch wood shakes, twice the size of shingles, from the yellow cedar trees, which covered the sides and roof. A hole was cut in the roof for a chimney. A canopy was built over the hole to keep out inclement weather; the fire was built on the floor directly under it. With feet pointing toward the fire, fifteen guests might sleep encircling it every night. Each family, however, did their own cooking. Dried salmon was split down the back and deboned, and then toasted.** The heat brings out the fat and oil in the fish so necessary to the Indian diet. The salmon is then dunked in seal grease, which is as bitter as caster oil, and then eaten with bread which had been baked in the open fire.

I, at last, enjoyed even the taste of seaweed. At low tide, in canoes with dogs for ballast, we'd gather seaweed into the canoes. The squaws would stomp forcibly on the seaweed then sit on it. This was a continuous process until the canoes could hold no more.

The seaweed, after being brought in, was spread to dry in piles four feet high. After it was stomped on again, all that remained was a cake that resembled a plug of chewing tobacco. While they wove, the squaws chewed on the salty seaweed until it swelled up and completely filled their mouths. Then they would toss it into a kettle. When the kettle was full, they added

---

* Clan law almost demanded open hospitality.

** A five-pound salmon dried in the rafters would, when dehydrated, be about one quarter of an inch thick. The fish were packed in bundles of fifty and stacked in the rafters for the winter supply.

water and herring eggs or salmon eggs, boiled it, and presto, a feast.

With a big mountain sheephorn spoon, each Indian would dip in for a spoonful of seaweed and pass the spoon to the next person, and thereon, to the time when the whole house had consumed enough. Notwithstanding the fact that the seaweed had been well-chewed first by the squaws, and that about fifty percent of the Indians had tuberculosis, I still found this dish very edible.

The berries that I had survived on, and which overloaded the islands, had to be preserved for the winter. It was the squaws' job to go out with blankets which they laid under a bush, bend the bush over and beat the berries off, into the blankets. They carried back tremendous loads, fifty pounds to the basket, and lined them up in the wind to blow away most of the leaves and sticks. We used to eat all the fresh berries we could at the time (and how I longed for a little cream and sugar). Then the berries were packed in seal or bear grease in the baskets and stored. It was not uncommon to see a squaw take a portion over to some neighbor who did not have such a delicacy, although the berries could be in a high state of putrefaction.

The most distasteful food of all, to me, was the salmon heads. Millions of salmon came to spawn in the creeks and rivers, so thick with them you couldn't row a boat through, so thick you could lay a plank across them and never submerge the plank. Even the bear came down by the dozen to feast. It was no trouble to kill the bear for food but the skins were not prime at that time of the year.

The Indians would catch the salmon, break the heads off several hundred, dig a hole in the beach at low tide, then line it with skunk cabbage leaves and fill the hole with fresh salmon heads. They tucked the outsize leaves around the heads, placed rocks on top and let the tide wash back and forth across them for about a week. When the hole was opened, everyone dug in and ate the heads which were rotten and stinking. The greatest delicacy of the feast, to the Indians, was the eye which they sucked out in the belief it would improve their own eyesight.

I have been able to stomach a bite from the nose of a live salmon, if I was ravenous when on a long hunting trip, and it wasn't too bad as gristle goes; but as long as I lived with the Indians I refused fish heads, despite my possibly offending them.

About every three months a steamer came with supplies for the single trading post in the village. There was no wharf. The steamer anchored out in the bay and unloaded the food supplies onto a barge which was then transported to the Kake Trading and Packing Company. In my later travels, through hearsay the K.T.&P. Company was jestingly referred to as the Kake Thieving and Plundering Company because all exchanges with the Indians were paid off in tin money, which could be redeemed only at the post. One time the steamer crew brought word that the lighthouse tender from Five Finger Island was coming to visit the Russian, Fred Stempovitch, who was in charge of the trading post, for a hunting expedition. To see visitors was always a great event for the Indians.

It was a stormy day when the lone man sailed over in his government lighthouse boat, but he tacked well against a strong head wind and after a perfect landing, came up to the trading post to meet with Mr. Stempovitch. I made an attempt to greet him but the Indians quickly whisked me back into the crowd.

The two men left on the hunting trip. It wasn't any chore to get game; all kinds were available between the islands.

The weather had turned calm, yet the two men absolutely disappeared. Rewards were offered but no one would search for the pair. A government compass was found in one Indian camp, a gun in another camp, boots in a third, and so on. No one ever knew what happened but I always heard the same story from the Indians — the Cushtaka got them both.

If the two white men had invaded the private property of the Indians, then it might be presumed that, as alien to the Indian laws regarding the right of ownership, the men were killed as poachers. Indians marked trees indicating property lines and the encroaching white hunters often tore down those signs or other markings in an attempt to take over the land for trapping purposes.

It was generally a sad day when the white man smugglers beached in with their sloops or schooners. They would drop off many gallons of whiskey in exchange for the skins they coveted, then depart leaving drunken Indians fighting and butchering each other.

One Indian, who had exhausted all his food supplies, spent all the skins he owned to the trading post for whiskey. In turn, the post cut off his account and would give him nothing more to eat. In a rage, he lashed his knife to the end of a long home-made spear and went to a cave where he knew a bear was hibernating. He burned his shirt on the end of a pole which he stuck inside the cave, to smoke the bear out. The bear's feet were tender after mouthing and sucking them all winter, and it stood bewildered and blinking on the frozen snow. Jim stepped up quickly and killed him with the spear. He dragged the carcass to the village, skinned it out and demanded food and his gun at the trading post. This was a kind of hardship wrought on the Indians as a result of the whiskey smugglers.

One steamer trip brought in a white American, Harry Pride, from Juneau. He had purchased a concession on an island about twenty-five miles from Kake, suitable for the raising of blue fox, of which he had twenty pair. My Indian father and another

65

hired fellow aided Pride in transferring the animals to the island, and I went along as a helper.

We caught halibut for the feed, then staked the halibut heads to the ground inside the portable pen of the foxes. For a while, they thrived but then began to waste away. Huge bald American eagles, we soon discovered, with wingspreads of six to eight feet, were swooping in and eating the fish. Hissing loudly, they would beat their wings, forcing the fox back from the food. Two or three eagles stood guard, spitting and fanning, while the others ate.

My job was to kill the intruders. Ish, who was a good hunter and an excellent shot, had taught me well how to handle a rifle. I shot several hundred and made my first money, a tidy stake at twenty-five cents a claw. Once, coming back from one of the fox island trips, I ran into a storm threatening to blow me out to sea, so I made a landing on a graveyard island a few miles from Kake. I wrapped myself in the old blankets used to adorn the graves and slept the night out. Those blankets, which fascinated me, were made of bark fibers and each fiber was wrapped in mountain sheep wool. They were fringed and had the totem figure of the deceased woven into the fabric. When the Indians heard I had slept in the graveyard, they were quite convinced I would bring the evil spirits, but again Ish assured them they had nothing to fear.

I showed the Indians the United States money I had received from the fox man for killing the eagles, but they didn't think it was good money. Only tin money was good!. I remember the prices paid for prime furs to the Indians. Mink was three dollars, six for marten, fur seal brought five dollars, hair seal one dollar, big bear skins eight dollars and a six-foot or more brown bear sold for ten dollars.

We hunted and trapped throughout the seasons but the main occupation on the island was salmon fishing. Ish captained his own fishing boat, a crew of seven, with the captain and six oarsmen manning eight-foot oars. We stood up, pushing the oars rather than sitting backwards to row. All the salmon habits were known. In the fish camp, look-outs were kept and everyone took turns watching the water in the bay. If a salmon was ready to spawn he'd jump playfully in the air, flip his tail, and fall back into the water. Whenever the salmon jumped, the alarm was spread, and we would hurry to the boats and put forth with all speed. If the salmon were just passing by, they would leave the water at an angle and dive back in. We didn't heed the angled jumpers because the whole school would be gone before we could get the nets in the water.

We knew the straight-out jumpers were there for a while, and as the boats circled them, one man would throw the purse-seine off with the lead lines on the bottom and the cork line on top.

It was no trick to pull up five thousand fish at one haul. Many times the nets were so full, half of the load was dumped out to keep the boat from capsizing. The Indians divided the salmon earnings at the end of the season and spent the money at the trading post for winter supplies.*

We lived a never-changing routine of eating and working from one season to the next. We were never hungry but I often yearned for a banana, an orange or an apple, and some sugar. Potatoes were unheard of. We had herb tea but no coffee.

During these years I was relegated to doing a man's work and had no companions my own age. Life left no time for "play." I was confined to my own family, and my only recreation was in listening to the elders relate their tales of prowess in battles.

The old chief of the Tlingit tribe of Kake Indians was called

---

* Salmon pay: Three quarters of a cent for a three-pound humpback salmon, a cent and a half for six-pound dog salmon, and seventy-five dollars a thousand for the Cohoe and Sockeye salmon.

Toskanatooktootletch. He used to sit by the fire, circled by other clansmen, and describe the great battles with other tribes. His greatest joy was to relate the battle with the Russian gunboat, which had come in to find survivors of a shipwreck. The Russians believed the Kakes had captured them — and the Indians knew the survivors had been taken by Custaka. The Russians shelled the village, leaving only the trading post standing and sent troops ashore to chase the Indians into the woods. As the Russians ran through the thick jungle, the Indians picked them off one by one, took their guns, and ran the rest off.

To rib the old chief a little, I would tell him about the American gunboats. "Our gunboats are not like those of the Russians. We carry two thousand men on ours. A boat as big as a village and they have guns that shoot fifty miles and kill all the people in the village with one shot." The old man would get very upset and walk away. He refused to listen to any nonsense that any other nation could be stronger than his.

The Kake Indians were proud fighters who fought many battles with opposing tribes, upon which they looked with scorn. Tribal wars were frequently caused by the enemy robbing traps, invading property or falsely claiming land. Settlement might be in the exchange of slaves and if the slaves were not satisfactory, the war would be continued.

It was only after the adoption ceremony that I knew positively I was a prisoner of the Kakes and my previous fears of the dreaded tribe were all unnecessary. The ferocity or savagery of the Kakes, as the prevalent belief was at that time, may have been rumored by all ships' captains, possibly as a preventive measure to keep sailors from jumping ship. The Kakes were proud, perhaps, but not savage! My life with eight hundred supposedly cruel Indians was an enriching one for two and a half years. I was treated and respected like a man.

RETURN TO CIVILIZATION

At a hundred yards distance in a strong wind, two trappers shouted at me that an earthquake had destroyed San Francisco six months before. That's how well informed I was concerning matters going on in the states. My first opportunity to get a letter to the mainland was through the fox man, Harry Pride, when I had been about six months with the Indians.

The mail boats arrived twice a year at the Point Ellis cannery, bringing in orientals to work the salmon pack. A mail boat came in while I was still in the village of Quatahein. I received an answer to a letter I had written to my brother, Clive, and my Aunt Dora in Denver, Colorado. They encouraged me to try to come home. My brother wanted me to help him start a pie factory.

I discussed the letter with my Indian father and told him I should leave when the steamer came in again. I offered to pay him back the amount he had paid for me, but he said I must remain with him. He had found a beautiful girl for me as a wife and I was to be married into the tribe, and, if I wanted, by the white man's legal way, too. He'd give me all his property, his canoes, guns — everything, and set me up in the trapping and fishing business, if I stayed.

I insisted I should go home and for the first time I saw in his face displeasure with me. He was adamant. I belonged to him, I was his son, and I could not leave.

At seventeen, having a tenacious mind of my own, I resolved to be on the steamer when it left. There were dozens of Indians on the wharf when the steamer returned. I watched the loading of the salmon until it was nearly completed, then I went up the coast in a canoe, waited there for low water, then paddled back to the steamer and climbed aboard on a fish ladder. I collided with the quartermaster, made a run for the stern and down a flight of stairs to the "Glory Hole" or the waiters' quarters where they were all having a "siesta."

Here, in full Indian costume and covered with pitch to ward off mosquitoes, I let out a blood-curdling yell.

The waiters rose to their feet as one man, stared at me and fled. They pushed and fell and slid under the bunks, under the tables, into the lockers, and out the door. Throughout the tumult I pleaded that I was the one to be afraid, and they at last believed me and hid me in the soap locker.

The beautiful engines rumbled and we started to move. I had made good my leave but not without incident. An hour later, the soap locker banged open and there stood the captain, resplendent in blue serge, gold braid, and brass buttons. With him was the purser.

"What the hell are you doing here, you savage?" he roared.

"I'm white," I said with dignity.

"The hell you are. You don't look white to me!"

"I am."

"Where are you from then, white man?"

"Nebraska," I retorted.

"You are in Alaska, not Nebraska."

"I said Nebraska. I am from Nebraska." The Captain, turning to what appeared to be a purplish hue, demanded my name.

I couldn't resist saying: "Kawoo Ketchtooyack."

The captain was in a towering rage by this time. It was against the law to take an Indian out of Alaska, and, confound it, he wasn't going to put back to port. He'd shove me overboard in a rowboat first. Then the purser asked me confidingly: "Are you a white man?"

"Yes, I am. My name is Senter. Gano Senter." The captain regained his composure and asked how I had come up to the Point. I told him I had been shanghaied on a sailing vessel three years ago. He queried the name of the ship and its destination.

He looked at the purser in surprise and said: "By heavens, I know this kid! I was the captain of the *Alki* that brought the *Agenor* supplies aboard and this kid tried to stow away then. He's all right; give him a ticket!"

I went topside and had a bath and a haircut, got depitched and deloused and dressed in clothes given me by the crew, who in turn fought over my Indian clothes for souvenirs. The captain invited me to sit at his table, an honor with which I was not familiar. The ladies, a group of school teachers at the table, also, fussed over me so much that I forgot my English and my manners. I was embarrassed. I bolted my meal and took refuge back down in the foc'sle with the sailors. I was eating with them when I was called out on deck by the captain. I apologized and then told him of my life with the Indians. He then took me to the officers' dining room where on the tables were bowls of fruit, raisins and nuts. I waded in and the captain ordered a waiter to feed me anything!

I ate and ate until I bulged. The captain left me alone and I couldn't believe my luck. I stuffed oranges in my shirt and other fruits in my pockets, but the captain had returned and commanded that I put everything back. He took me up to a stateroom adjoining his own and called a waiter to fill several fruit bowls, and said if they were ever found empty, the waiter would be put ashore.

Word got around about my amazing past. Among the two hundred passengers was a writer for the *Elmira Telegram* and *Outlook* magazine of Seattle. He wanted an interview, but I left that up to the captain and he decided "no reporters."

A wireless was sent ahead to Seattle to report that I was off the *Agenor* and was aboard. When we docked, the captain personally escorted me to the Ferrin Hotel and left me while he went on personal business. He returned the next day to find a gang of newspaper reporters in my room, posing as a ship's crew. It was too late to stop them from taking pictures of me. Gory and untrue stories were published. (One article actually showed a picture of a squaw, whom, the article conjectured, I was forced to bring with me.)

The captain sensibly asked what my future plans were and offered me a berth on his ship. I had no plans, but I also did not want to go back to Denver at this time. I signed on as a crew member and made many trips to Alaska with the captain, but never again into Kake Indian country. I did, however, serve as interpretor for passengers with the border Indians.

On one trip to Seattle I hired an express wagon to carry my gear to my room ashore. The driver of the wagon took one look at me and jumped as if he had seen a ghost. "My God, you're Senter." It was Slim, the Kansas farmer.

We talked about the *Agenor* and he handed me a clipping which said the ship had made Yokohama in one hundred and two days. The salmon had rotted and the ship given up as lost. Two men had died on the way to Japan; the ship was scuttled in Kobe Bay for $108,000 insurance; three men went down in her; and the captain and mate were imprisoned for life.[*]

Slim said he had been part of the search party sent out to find Harry and me. The found the ship's boat capsized and smashed on a reef, and since the Indians had all left the area, they figured that we had no doubt drowned. Before the ship embarked for Japan, Slim managed an escape on Captain Olsen's gasoline launch. As far as he knew, we were the only two survivors of the *Agenor* crew.

---

[*] This article was printed in January, 1906.

PART TWO

THE FISHERMAN

I was loafing around the waterfront in Wrangell, Alaska, when I heard about a halibut schooner that was short one man. I hunted up the captain, a big, sturdy Scandinavian. He examined me in a glance and said: "You're pretty damned small." I answered: "Yeah, but I'm pretty damned strong."

A halibut schooner usually carried an auxiliary engine, in addition to her sails and four to six dories, plus a crew considered the roughest and toughest of all seafaring men. With two men to a dory, nobody was anxious to take on a newcomer as a partner because of his inexperience. But as the pay depended upon the total number of fish caught, every man was obliged to do his share. The captain received a sixty per cent profit from the sales of the catch, and the remaining forty was divided among the crew members.

A twelve man crew aboard, we left the dock on the four o'clock fair tide the next morning. Our course was set for the halibut banks about forty miles out to sea.

I was paired off with a huge six foot, two hundred and fifty pound Finn. We both dressed in sou'westers, slickers, rubber boots and heavy woolen mittens. We had a keg of smelt for bait and several skates of gear. This consisted of a heavy line a hundred fathoms long with six-inch hooks on a six-foot drop line set every fifteen-feet apart.

While one man rowed, the other baited the hooks with smelt and cast the line off the stern. The gear which was cast overboard had an anchor on the bottom and a keg buoy with a flag on it on the top so the setup could be found later.

After putting off the first skate gear, we proceeded along to number two, three and four gears. We circled back to check lines in an hour or so and to pull in our catch. The halibut was hit on the head with a heavy pine-knot club and hauled in with a hay-hook. Sometimes we would pull in fifteen to twenty halibut from each gate, ranging in size from two to five feet each. When the boat was loaded to the gunnels, it was regarded as an excellent fishing day, then we'd sit and wait for the mother ship to come and pick us up at night.

The vessel's davits would swing out and one of us on each end of the boat would hook on and we'd be hoisted aboard. Regardless of weather or size of catch, we always had to unload, gut our fish, and stow them away in tanks in the lower hold. Then we would thaw out our frozen oilskins and mittens, kick off our boots, and go into the foc'sle for dinner.

Our catch was always good. I was also pleased with the treatment received aboard ship. I was convinced this was the job for me — until a change came one morning.

We awoke to a heavy overcast, and as we were swung out and dropped into the water, the skipper announced that the barometer was low. About noon it began to drizzle and sleet and our oilskins were covered with spray, frozen by the icy wind. My partner rowed while I pulled in a fine catch. One five footer I had clubbed came to life while I was manning an oar to help pull to the next gear, and walloped me with his tail, knocking me to the other end of the boat.

My mittens, slick with fish slime and gurry, made it impossible to hold onto the oar, so I rowed bare-handed in the freezing temperature. Our gear fouled up and we had to cut part of that away and lost time in trying to untangle it. The boat shipped water and with our load we couldn't bail. The big Finn cursed and cried over each fish he threw overboard. It was getting darker and there was no sign of the mother ship. We couldn't light the lantern because our fingers were frostbitten. Then the winds came and all our resourcefulness and skill as seamen were demanded as our main concern now was to keep afloat.

The mother ship had picked up all the other fishermen and she was making great circles with her searchlight to spot us. Once she came within hailing distance, but with the wind sweeping across the ship's direction, our calls were lost and the light missed us. We were tossed and buffeted by the gale. To keep from freezing, we'd pull against the wind now and again, keeping our body circulation going.

Shortly before midnight, we saw again the slender finger of light coming, circling and searching. Drenched and nearly frozen, we were hauled aboard with half a load. That time we didn't have to clean the fish. The mother ship had a capacity load and we put back to Port Wrangell.

A large crowd had gathered on the dock to welcome us. We had to do some fancy tacking to come in with the strong head wind. It was Big Ole's job to let down the jib, which he commenced to do without special orders. The captain shouted in his lusty voice: "Ole, damn your salty hide, don't let down the yib until I say let down the yib! . . . Ole . . . let down the yib!" I ended my halibut fishing career with a good laugh and a good bit of money.

THAR SHE BLOWS

"How would you like to go whaling?" was the question. I replied I knew nothing about whaling.

"They seldom harpoon from a boat anymore," he said. "Now they have modern steel, steamship vessels with harpoon guns."

I was a drifter, eighteen, and out of Petersburg one time, when I was talking to a group of Indians in the Tlingit dialect about the halibut fishing. Several curious white men gathered around to listen, and, somehow, the conversation turned to whaling. The man who started the discussion was looking for help and as he talked, the idea of whaling became more appealing to me, enough to join the crew of the *Tyee Jr.*

We were transported in a gasoline launch to "Murder Cove" where the whales were processed. Docking there, the foreman informed us that the steamer was still out to sea and we would have to work in the station until the ship returned.

It was the most modern whaling station of its day. A huge smokestack reared up into the sky; three hundred-foot slips made of wood sloped down into the water; and there were bone crushing machines and tremendous vats and retorts plus a very large crane with a lifting capacity of many tons.

I was handed a razor-sharp, three-foot knife fastened to the end of a six-foot pole. Three other men were similarly equipped. We were escorted to a slip where lay a sixty-foot whale. The foreman marked places for us to begin cutting. We cut slabs two-feet wide and six-feet long across the whale. One man climbed up on a catwalk and reaching with his knife, cut the center slab holding the meat together. Each of us reached up with a long-handled hook and gave a slab a yank while the man on top separated the meat from the bone. With a crash, down came a three hundred-pound piece of whale meat at our feet. A dozen slabs at a time were hauled by winch to the retort for processing.

It took several days of cutting to expose the whale's skeleton and the stench was horrible. The Alaska mosquitoes and flies swarmed over the meat and blood. The great carcass was removed to the bone pile by the crane with its big hooks. Bones stacked fifty-feet high were crushed by machine for fertilizer, and the commercial bones sorted out for corset stays and various uses.

If the season was good there would be at least three whales floating in the bay waiting processing. The whale was towed in by boat, hooks driven in on either side of the head, and on signal from the winch driver, everyone would jump clear of the big cables. We'd watch the monster being pulled gradually up to the cutting dock where the cutting operation was repeated.

I was happy when the *Tyee Jr.* arrived at the end of that week. She unloaded her catch and took us aboard.

The captain put me up in the crow's nest since I was a greenhorn. "All you've got to do, sonny, is keep your eyes open every minute and when you see a whale you shout in a loud voice, 'Thar she blows' and point in the right direction. Now let's hear you try!"

In what I thought was a loud cry, I shouted: "Thar she blows!" Everyone laughed. The captain called over a sailor to demonstrate for me and then told me to practice on deck. "We want to hear your voice whichever way the wind is blowing."

I saw a whale that next day. I mustered all the lung power I could and sang out: "Thar she blows!" and I pointed west. They heard me and the orders flew out immediately. "Gunner, man your guns — all hands on deck." The crew of four men in number one boat swung over the side. The gunner manned his station and extra ropes and buoys were readied. The captain gave bell signals to the engine room — SLOW. When we were within gunshot range he changed course to broadside the whale. The engines were slowed again to barely moving. The whale was resting easy. The order to fire was given and the decks quivered as the harpoon left its gun. "Bull's eye!" came the cry. Ropes, coiled in barrels so they wouldn't tangle, looped through the air. As the harpoon found its mark, the whale hit the water with his tail and disappeared.

I had been so intent on following the actions of the number one boat, which rowed nearby waiting for the whale to surface, that I almost missed seeing a second whale blow, in the opposite direction. Again I puffed up and sang out. The course was changed and the second boat was manned. The harpoon missed the target but caught the moving whale toward his stern. Another shot had to be fired when whale and ship were in position. Meanwhile the number one boat had located its whale and dropped an anchor and a barrel buoy at the place while the navigator took bearings and marked a chart. The second whale surfaced for air several times but always in a different direction so we had to wait and watch. When the whale submerged himself in a reef of shallow water, the whale boat was ordered out.

Mr. Hansen, the first mate, and the only man aboard who could throw a harpoon, took his place in the bow as the whale boat approached the reef and the partly submerged whale. The harpoon was in position with carefully coiled rope in a sawed-off barrel. At Hansen's signal, the oarsmen rowed silently toward the whale who might have been asleep, crippled, or dead. Fifteen feet off, the mate stood up, lifted the heavy harpoon and with a mighty heave plunged the instrument into the whale. The rope flew out with a buoy on the end. The whale plunged and churned the water dark with blood, disappeared then re-appeared. I was tense as I watched from the deck. I saw the boat rise up into the air with the whale coming up directly under the boat's bow. A man spilled out of the stern and another reached for him with a boat hook. The whale submerged and the boat was caught in a whirlpool but fortunately did not get sucked under. Ten minutes elapsed and the whale floated to the surface dead. An anchor and buoy were attached to it and we departed.

We steamed into Taku Bay at sundown, dropped anchor, and enjoyed the awesome spectacle of the Taku glaciers, a favorite tourist stop. Here it was a custom of the captains to give several short blasts of the ship's whistle which caused thousands of tons of ice to break off and slide down the glacier walls to the sea, creating waves fifteen feet high.

Imagine our joy the next morning to see four whales inside the bay, playing, spouting, diving, and splashing around us. It was difficult to know which whale to go after first until one surfaced not fifty yards from the ship. The gunner fired a bull's eye and the whale went to the bottom with a tremendous splash of his tail and down came the glacier walls, followed by a thundering roar of falling ice. The waves caught us broadside knocking everyone flat. Confusion reigned and the longboat, about to be launched, filled with water. The second boat went out to anchor and buoy our whale. The rest of the whales departed Taku Bay and all the commotion.

One of the fishermen had been injured and I exchanged places with him. The crow's nest for the ship's crew.

Three days later we came upon two more whales. We were steaming along toward our number one whale when the captain ordered soundings be taken. Charts were consulted and disclosed our coming into a reef barrier. Under SLOW bells we cautiously pulled out into deep water, getting within killing range of the whales. The fire command was anticipated just as the first whale submerged. We waited breathlessly, wondering where to look, when the lookout spotted the whale going in the opposite direction, and toward the second whale. The ship's course was changed and we had two whales in the target. We approached slowly and heard: "Thar she blows!" and "Fire!"

The whales broke and plunged, one mortally wounded. Suddenly the *Tyee* heaved and we all went down, to the sound of grinding and groaning of ship's timbers.

We were on the reef. The order came to shut the bulkheads and to launch the whaleboat. The captain seemed unperturbed and said we'd sail at high tide and in the meantime: "Get out there and mark that whale!"

At high tide we floated gently off the reef and back into familiar, deep water. We towed the last whale out of the reef barriers and then retraced our course to pick up the other whales. We had killed four in ten days. Upon our return to Murder Cove, I decided to let someone else do the butchering. I resigned from my vocation as a whaler.

GOLD FEVER

From Seattle I shipped on the steamship *Dolphin*, as a deck hand. She was transporting more than one hundred passengers to the Klondike, of whom several were making a repeat trip. It was 1909; the Alaskan gold rush was still going strong and they intended to strike it rich this visit. I, too, was bitten by the gold-fever bug. When we reached Skagway, the end of the route for the Inside Passage and jumping-off place for the Yukon, I quit the ship to take on the challenge.

I had some money but not enough to buy a boat and supplies. I joined forces with Joe Miller and Bill Wood, and the three of us walked the White Pass Trail from Skagway to Whitehorse, a distance of one hundred and eleven miles.

It took us a week, and along the way we found gold seekers strung out on the trail, too exhausted to move on. At times we'd stumble over discarded cooking utensils, supplies, and guns, the last possession a man would discard — then, we would find the man. His plea for help had to be ignored; only the fittest survived, in that country, at that time. It was a harrowing experience.

At Whitehorse we acquired a boat in need of repair but one we could afford to buy at thirty dollars each. At a ships' chandlery hardware store we bought a bolt of caulking and caulking compound, and drove it all into the boat seams, adding also white lead, and then we painted the boat.

We bought what we considered sufficient food at the general

store at a total cost of one hundred and fifty dollars. The opening of the Yukon River's ice usually occurred on May twenty-fifth. A great deal of betting went on, as to when the ice would go out. That year the ice opened on the twenty-sixth and the stampede to get down the river began. We climbed into our fourteen-foot boat with our grubstake and gear amidst the warnings of bystanders. One old timer said: "You won't get very far in those rapids. Go get yourselves a tree and hang it onto the end of your boat." On his advice, we cut a thirty-foot tree and tied it securely to the stern of the boat.

We realized why we needed it when we hit the rapids — it was a brake for the boat.

Off we went through the swirling torrent of boiling, raging water. We pushed and shoved frantically to keep off the rocks, using three oars to keep us from being smashed to a pulp. We hit boulders and bounced high in the air, came down on the beam and spun like a pinball. At the bottom of the rapids, we were catapulted into a whirlpool and gyrated like a top until we were shot out into the peaceful Yukon River again.

We pulled ashore and made camp, cooked a supper of bacon and beans, and pitched our battered, leaky old tent, to recover from shooting the rapids. Other gold rushers arrived, and we all sat around a fire until early morning, exchanging hair-raising tales of those rapids. Plenty of "shooters" hadn't lived to tell their stories, so we felt somewhat lucky and secure.

Klondike gold was the magic word that influenced thousands of men from all over America to head for the barren wastelands of Alaska. If they could make it, all prospectors followed a course leading directly to Dawson. When we reached Dawson, we discerned discouragement on every side; the gold had been gobbled up by the large companies.

Just before we came, a herd of several thousand caribou had passed through one edge of town and demolished many of the prospectors' shacks. Nothing can alter the course of the caribou on the move! The Indians and Eskimos had killed many of them, however. Some men were foolish enough to shoot into the fore-ranks of the stampeding herd and the downed animals were reduced to fragments. Experienced hunters waited until the herd had passed and then bagged the animals in the rear, providing themselves with enough meat for a month.

After hearing of the sad cases of hardships and privations, we decided that Fairbanks would be a better place to risk our few dollars.

Before leaving Whitehorse, the three of us had agreed upon a set of working rules; sharing the necessary cooking, hustling for wood, etcetera, but the further we traveled together, the more arguments we got into. At the end of three weeks, when we reached Fairbanks, we were glad to disband, each to go his own way.

FAIRBANKS

Horny-handed sons of toil, bearded, dirty, ragged prospectors and miners, dog teams and merchants — all swarmed the streets of Fairbanks. The lucky ones weighed in gold to buy drinks for the "have-nots" at the Horseshoe Saloon on Main Street. Nightly, the sawdust on the floor of the saloon yielded about one hundred and fifty dollars from gold dust, dropped from the miner's poke and off the scales. The sweepers used a fine broom on the floor, and even floated sawdust in tubs of water so the gold would settle to the bottom. The take was often more than the miner himself was making with pick and shovel.

An old fellow related his sorrow one night in the saloon to earn himself a drink. With arms waving and eyes popping he recited "The Miner's Lament."

You know son, I've panned from Peru to Point Barrow,
But I never located a claim
Until I persuaded my conscience
That pay dirt pervaded the same.
This is the source of my sorrows,
As you will be forced to agree
When you learn how relentless misfortune
Has dumped all her tailings on me.
I worked with my partner all summer
Crosscutting a cussed cold creek
Which we never once thought we would locate
Unless we located the streak
And when at the close of the season,
We discovered the creek was a fake,
We also discovered the region
Had nothing left in it to stake.
So we went a hundred long leagues to the Northward

O'er the downtrodden, sun-burnished snow,
We struggled half blinded — half famished
To the sea where the staunch whalers go.
We came upon beaches of rubies
With mountains and placers and leads.
But all save the sky was preempted by
Salt water, sailors and Swedes.
So we climbed the cold creeks near a mission
That is run by the agents of God,
Who trade Bibles and prayerbooks to heathens
For sealskin, ivory and cod.
At last we were sure we had struck it,
But alas for our hope of reward,
The landscape from seabeach to skyline
Was staked in the name of the Lord.
Yes, we're too slow for this new breed of miners,
Embracing all classes of men,
Who locate by power of attorney
And prospect their claim with a pen.
Who do all their fine work through agents
And loaf around town with the sports.
They're on intimate terms with the lawyers
And on similar terms with the courts.

I bought him a drink.

In Fairbanks, the rich got richer, the poor, poorer, and I was among the latter. I didn't have sufficient funds to buy a grubstake or tools to go on a prospecting journey, even if I had had the nerve and the know-how.

It was back to work for me. I accepted a job walking ditch for a mining company which paid the grand sum of ten dollars a day and board. That was big money for a young buckaroo like me.

At night I came into town to see the bright lights, watch the gambling and the shooting between over excited and overly drunk brawlers, and I can never forget the dog fights. Two dogs would attack each other and fifteen more circled the pair, waiting until one of the contestants went down, then the others would rush in and tear the loser to ribbons. It was in Fairbanks I learned what the expression "dog eat dog" meant.

I was on the move again and lucky to catch a ride on a paddle-wheeler going down the river to St. Maechel. There I had the good fortune to find a tramp freighter named the *Ella*. She needed a deck hand for the ports of Nome and Koodsiboo Sound, Point Barrow and the in-between stops. I was headed for the Arctic Circle.

LAND OF THE MIDNIGHT SUN

The *Ella* proved to be a staunch, seaworthy iron ship with a good crew, good officers, and, above all, good food. I often compared this ship with some of the terrible tramps I had sailed on.

It was a bright and sunny day when we sailed into Point Barrow, yet it was the most desolate, barren, uninviting place I could remember visiting in all my travels.

In the harbor were half a dozen Arctic whalers riding at anchor and two tramp steamers. There were six white men and perhaps a hundred Indians in the village. The Hudson Bay Trading Post dealt in all the necessities of northern life.

Since there wasn't any wharf, a barge was sent out to load and unload the ship. The Eskimos whom I often bartered with at ports-of-call did the freight handling. I'd trade butter for their carved walrus ivory. I've seen them build an igloo in a couple of hours and watched with interest when they slopped dried salmon boiled with bran out on the snow for the dogs, who lapped it up, then dug their hole in the snow to go to sleep. And there at Point Barrow I saw the Eskimos gazing longingly at the calico, perfumed soap, and beads — added victims of the white man's civilization.

During the day, the village was quiet, but at night the action flowered. The one saloon bulged with cutthroats and roughneck sailors of every nationality, including Russians who wore beards and carried long knives. On the surface, the atmosphere was one of hilarity and friendliness, but we could always expect a good brawl when mariners started to compare and brag about their ships. Eventually, it would get down to personalities and individual bravery, and then the fists would fly.

Their method of fighting was similar to the dog fights. A gang circled two opponents, waited until one man went down, and then a general free for all would begin, where everyone "moved in for the kill." The onlookers now divided into four or five smaller groups to fight each other. Afterwards, the wounds were nursed and another round of drinks bought. When it was all over, the participants staggered aboard their ships declaring another victory for the common people.

These mariners usually blew all their money the first night or two ashore. Then they looked forward to the arrival of a trapper with a sled load of skins to cash in, then the party and the brawl could be repeated.

The seaman who could come back aboard his ship with the most cuts and bruises and the one who could get rolled and robbed and come back broke, was the hero among his shipmates during the next voyage. The stories have got to be good on ship or shore.

WALRUS

A group of Eskimos came alongside the freighter and I engaged a roly-poly Eskimo named Ayack in conversation. I spoke to him in Tlingit Indian and he answered me in Eskimo. Neither of us could understand the other but we kept trying.

I paused for breath and asked Ayack: "You savvy English?"

He shut his eyes and grinned. "I not only understand English but I teach English in my native school."

Ayack invited me ashore to have tea with him in his igloo. I was on duty and couldn't leave the ship. The first mate, who had been listening to us, asked to speak to Ayack. He was very eager to hunt a walrus, and since the ship was laying in for a few days for engine repair, now would be his opportunity if he had a guide. Ayack said he would be glad to take anyone who had guns. His brother, a nomad, was visiting him and he hunted walrus with a spear. The mate made arrangements immediately for us to leave the ship.

We stopped by Ayack's "igloo," a shack made of packing boxes, for tea and dried walrus meat dipped in seal grease. We choked it down and Ayack insisted we had better eat heartily because we might have to drag a half-ton walrus back with us. We were instructed to remove our shoes and wear his knee-high walrus hide boots. It was only two hours to the hunting grounds, they said, and we should be there at half tide. We'd have to work very fast to make a kill and get it back to the village by dark. The two Eskimos hitched up a dog team and while they called "Mush, mush on" and "Way ha!" the five dogs strained against their harnesses. We ran alongside holding onto the sled for balance and to help the dogs pull over the bare patches.

We came to a little peninsula which on the north side sloped down into the ocean and with a side on the south offering us good protection. Leaving the sled, Ayack and his brother, Auteka, started across the tundra to the foot of a small reef rising out of the sea. The mate and I crawled on our hands and knees to the top of the reef and, peering over, beheld forty or fifty walruses. Ayack signaled us to take aim but not to fire until Auteka had cast his spear. Auteka, who had moved to within throwing distance, rose from his crouching position and threw his spear at a big bull walrus, and almost simultaneously we released the triggers of our guns. All of our shots were good and we had three walruses. Then pandemonium broke loose on the reef. Cows and calves screamed. The bulls bellowed and some started to charge us, but their defiance soon abated and they left the reef for the sea. We were now faced with the problem of towing the monsters, each weighing at least half a ton, behind the sled. On snow it was not too difficult to keep the sled moving, but over the barren patches we had a laborious task. We floated the walruses in the water around the shore the last part of the route, and then brought only one as far as the ship, which we transported aboard with block and tackle.

We made it back about dark and all the crew members came out on deck to view the great hunter, the first mate, who beamed with pride when the captain and officers inspected his kill.

We returned the next day to bring back the other two walruses. Ayack and Auteka demonstrated how to skin the walrus out and extract the tusks, so that not a pound of meat or an inch of skin would be wasted. Also, how to select the bones which were used for utensils and for carving. We left most of the skins and meat with the brothers but kept the tusks. In later years, I had mine made into a huge cribbage board.

INSIDE PASSAGE TO ALASKA

I was in Seattle again and signed on the passenger steamship *Jefferson*. One of our runs included sailing through the Straits of Juan de Fuca to British Columbia, Vancouver Island. Our first port-of-call was Prince Rupert. We docked and unloaded railroad ties, spikes, and building materials to be used for the beginning of the Canadian-Pacific Transcontinental Railroad.

Here I had my first venture in real estate. A salesman convinced four of us of the future potential of Prince Rupert. I paid ten dollars for a lot and received a receipt. I never returned to Prince Rupert but my ownership receipt entitled me at one time to sail on C-P Steamship Company ships in Canadian waters.

The next port for the *Jefferson* was the village of Methletathka, founded years before by a Scotchman named Father Duncan. The village was on Anet Island inhabited by the Methletathka Indians. White men were not welcome because Father Duncan did not want the white man's whiskey. All the attending vices would jeopardize the purpose of his mission. He had established fishing canneries, some of which are still in operation. When they heard me speak in the Indian tongue, I was honored to be one of the few white men to be welcomed ashore.

THE SEYMORE NARROWS

The Seymore Narrows was probably the most treacherous water known to navigation. It was so swift and so narrow that any wise captain would carefully set his sailing schedule to arrive there on slack tide. Misjudging of the tide had caused ships to be crushed against the narrow walls, ripping open hulls on the jagged rocks along the base. I had seen hundred-foot pine trees sucked under, not to reappear, or to be broken in splinters like matches in the current; or the water, instead of sucking the trees under, would spew them high into the air, so deceptive and mysterious was this bit of water.

We had one hundred head of cattle on board the *Jefferson* between decks. The cattle in rows were locked in stanchion with a feed trough at their heads and a manure trough at their sterns. It was my job to feed them, which I was doing, unaware of our position in relation to the Seymore Narrows whose waters I knew well. Previous voyages had always been so timed that we sailed safely through. I was pitching hay when, unexpectedly, the ship flipped on its side. I watched in horror as fifty cattle stood on their heads, broke their stanchion bars, and plunged across the feed trough plowing their horns into the unfortunate animals on the port side. At the same time, an eight-inch stream of water cascaded through each port hole with the velocity of a fire hose. Everything was swept to port side and the ship careened as if at any instant she would swamp and go under.

Abruptly the ship was righted and then flipped over on her other side. The bawling cattle were swept to starboard with horns tangling and stabbing. Their cries mingled with hysterical screams from passengers. Again the ship righted and it was all over. The currents swept us on through the Narrows to the calm water of the Inside Passage. It was rumored later that the captain had deliberately missed the slack tide in order to get rid of those cattle. He knew every current in the narrows.

The livestock were hooked with block and tackle and tossed overboard. The injured ones were shot and heaved over. At the end of this trip, the *Jefferson* relinquished the cattle business.

Our usual sailing schedule called for stops at Wrangell, Petersburg, Juneau, Douglass, Haines, Skagway and Sitka. Occasionally we made side trips into the island country to a remote cannery, and at these ports I'd stand on the foc'sle head and many times Indians would recognize me and spread the word that Kawoo was in town. I would go ashore with the tourists as an interpreter to help them shop for pottery, baskets, ivory, and Indian clothing.

GAMBLERS AND ORIENTALS

The passenger list of Alaskan steamers included businessmen, miners, tourists, and gamblers. The latter had a schedule, every fall and spring, the first and last trips they came aboard. Though they assured the passengers they played an honest game, they seemed capable of fleecing even the most experinced card sharks.

On one of these trips I had given the purser, for safekeeping, a considerable amount of money I had earned from my Arctic Circle trips. I told a ship's waiter of the purse, and shortly therafter, I was invited to sit in a blackjack game in the "Glory Hole." I increased my twenty-five dollars to one hundred that night, but the next evening I was feverishly playing with my savings. The dealer eventually gathered in my seven hundred dollars, and at Skagway the waiter took off his white jacket to join his other gambler buddies. From shore he waved affectionately to the young sucker, me. The professionals weren't always on deck, they also signed on as members of the ship's crew.

The steamship *Jefferson* took on board a hundred pig-tailed Chinese bound for work in an Alaska cannery. A few decks below water line, in steerage, they would lie in the high bunks with their little lamps and pipes, and smoke opium. A rolled up dab of opium was cooked over the lamp, stuffed into the pipe, and then puffed on, while their souls flitted away to heaven.

The Chinese were inveterate gamblers. Before the ship had docked and the card game was over and the smoke of battle and opium had cleared away, many of them would have hypothecated their season's unearned salaries to the winner. Half the group came to the cannery as captive workers, and half were destined to get fat on the earnings. If the loser did not pay his debt, the code of the gambling tongs would permit him to be assassinated.

On another voyage we carried a hundred Hindus, brown-skinned turbaned laborers. At sea they informed the ship's personnel that their religion would not permit eating food cooked or handled by the crew and begged to use the galley after hours. The permission was granted and we watched them make their own bread. In circle formation, each man offered a prayer as the dough was handed to him; he would give it a pat and pass it on. The dough was then laid on top of the range to bake slowly. With blessings from Buddha, they seasoned the food with curry and spices and had a banquet every night.

During a storm the Hindus lay prostrate from seasickness, on deck or in their quarters. All hope of living was abandoned. We would simply stack them up on top of each other, and off to one side. Other shipboard duties demanded our attention.

OCTOPUS

Sailing South, we stopped at a cannery to load some twenty thousand cases of salmon. Here I was invited by the natives to go out to the reefs and gather seaweed at low tide.

We sailed in a big canoe for about twenty miles, and I had an enjoyable time chatting about Indian customs and my experiences with the Kakes. At the reefs, we waded out for the edible seaweed and gathered in great armfuls. I suddenly slipped into deep water over the tops of the rubber hip boots I was wearing. In my struggle to pull out, I felt a lash whip my leg and discovered I was in the grasp of a ten-foot octopus. I saw him once and then the water turned inky black. I felt two more whip lashes as two more tentacles with suckers latched onto my boots. The pressure was great. The Indians attempted to pull my leg out of the boot, but my encumbrance was very weighty; my leg would come off first. The Indians teased and prodded the octopus until all the tentacles were wrapped around my leg and then, cut them off all at one stroke. We pulled the octopus up, still clasping my leg with one tentacle.

One of the Indians wielded the death blow as he plunged a knife into its head. I was grateful it had hooked onto my rubber boot instead of my skin, for the octopus could have bled me to death by sucking through my skin, that is, if he hadn't drowned me first. Needless to say, I have never cared for the delicacy since that experience.

DEPARTMENT STORE
TEDDY BEAR

I volunteered to talk to the Indians on the beach about duck hunting. The crews always desired to go hunting whenever they saw the sky turn black with game birds.

The Indians first suggested I go bear hunting with them and discuss the subject further.

Four dogs, barking and cavorting, led us into the forest and soon circled a black she-bear, cutting off her escape to a tree. They bit at her heels time and time again, keeping her rotating until she was dizzy. We couldn't call the dogs off before the bear made a pass at one dog, ripping a leg out of its socket. At the kill, the bear's two cubs came running, which, after some coaxing, we caught.

I brought the cubs back to the ship with me, to everyone's delight. The ship's carpenter built a pen for them and the cook contributed a baby bottle. I rigged some warm milk and hand-fed them on deck each day and they became the topic of conversation with the passengers.

After a heavy sea in Queen Chalotte Sound which made everyone seasick, including the animals, one of the cubs died. The female lived and by the time we docked at Seattle she was well-trained and friendly. I took her to my rooming house on Yeslerway to the amusement of the roomers and the consternation of the landlady, who, however, did loan me a dog kennel.

The cub played and romped with me just like a dog, and if she was cross would cry like a baby. The neighbors then accused me of beating her. Her name, Swipes, originated from her continual habit of swinging her paw at me.

At the Alaska-Yukon Exposition in Seattle at this time, I met a group of Eskimos and Tlingit Indians who were homesick to the point of real despair. They were physically sick as well because they could not get accustomed to the food. They yearned for bear grease, seal oil, and seaweed.

In my compassion, I went to the waterfront and secured an open berth on an Alaskan steamer leaving that same day for Indian country. I returned in two weeks with five five-gallon coal oil cans full of seal grease, a bale of seaweed, and some bundles of dried salmon. In their pleasure, I even joined them in eating, much to the dismay of the exposition tourists.

During those two intervening weeks, the department store manager of the Bon Marche, as an advertising gimmick, was keeping Swipes for me. He built her a pen in the front store window, and I was told great crowds gathered to watch Swipes play with the toys.

One evening after the store was closed, Swipes got loose and decided to go shopping. She first visited the material department and unwound the bolts of cloth and ribbon. Blouses, shirts, hats were all entangled in a big mess, from one end of the store to the other.

The manager called a council of war and it was unanimously recommended that bears were undesirable. My landlady and neighbors were also tired of her antics, and to save the bear from total destruction, I took her to the Woodland Park Zoo.

Ten years had drifted by when I took my wife and two daughters to Seattle and to the zoo where I stepped under a railing and over to a pacing bear, whom I was sure fitted Swipes' description. I called: "Swipes, come here!" She came forward and I thrust a button on my coat through the bars. She quickly sat on her haunches, put her front paws and snoot through the bars and started sucking as she had when she was weaned from the bottle. The zoo keeper, who was looking on, laughed and said he was convinced she was Swipes, but that they would continue to call her Molly.

SHIPWRECK

The craft *Altoona* was just an ordinary steamer with an ordinary crew and irregular sailing schedules. When I joined her, she was hauling freight to ports that other tramp ships did not make. Her crew comprised ten deck hands and a black gang of twelve firemen and coal passers. The black gang considered us deck sailors stupid for working top side where the icy gales froze our hands and feet. We faced the added danger of being swept overboard.

When I saw them come up from their warm room below in a state of total exhaustion, after feeding the engines twenty tons of coal a day, too tired to eat or sleep and twitching for hours in their bunks, I was glad to be on deck with cold hands and feet.

At eight bells one afternoon, I heard a commotion near the door of the engine room. I poked my head in and stared down into the face of a husky fireman hanging on the ladder. He had just come off duty and had climbed fifteen feet when he was stricken with cramps in his leg and both hands. He hung there, cursing and hollering, his half-naked body swing to and fro with the motion of the ship. Someone went down to him with a rope and pulled him up on deck.

On a steamer, the fireman was often considered the lowest member of the crew, all back and no brain. All he had to do was keep the pressure up and the ship moving, according to some. Yet, he might be lucky to get in a few puffs of his pipe in between pressure readings and flashing of the fires. Flashing the fire was done with an iron bar, ten feet long and three inches thick on one end and tapering down to one inch on the small end. The fireman broke up the clinkers accumulating in the furnaces and with a ten-foot long, hundred-pound rake pulled the biggest clinkers out onto the steel deck plates, where they hit with a crash. A hose was used to wet down the sparks that flew in all directions and everyone enjoyed a nice steam bath. The fireman then toted the clinkers in buckets to topside and dumped them overboard. He did these chores in four-hour shifts, four on and four off. When a ship carried a complement, we all welcomed the four hours on and eight hours off duty.

When the latter occurred, the black crew took baths and a few individuals even looked white again. One big fellow, Black Jack, said there wasn't any sense to cleaning up since he'd have to go back into the black hole. It was true, however, he did like his work below.

It was also fact that at times we did get washed overboard and a man or two would be lost when the boat swamped in the icy cold Arctic water. But at least we saw the blue sky, the sea gulls, and the porpoises.

"Listen, mate, when this ship hits a reef and is shipwrecked, you'll be the first to go overboard," prophesied Black Jack. And I quipped: "Yeah, what about you — bottled up down there in the bowels?" His reply to that was "a nice warm swim while you fellows on top will freeze."

The *Altoona* was not allowed to carry passengers because she flew a red flag, which meant she was a dynamite cargo ship loaded with powder, caps, and fuses for the mining industry. The captain was not adverse, however, to picking up a little extra fare from strangers who were unaware of this restriction. One trip we had four cheechakos.*

After leaving Dutch Harbor, all attention was focused on a

---

* Greenhorns who have never wintered in Alaska because they haven't enough money, or those who want to return to the states.

strange cloud approaching over the horizon on the starboard side. The cloud materialized into swarms of sea gulls who flew beyond us as we continued to chop along, southward.

When the midnight watch came on, we learned why the sea gulls were flying out to sea. In an instant the ship was buried in three-quarters of an inch of volcanic ash and cinders. A mantle of sulphur fog descended over the entire ship. I felt my eyes smart and my lungs hurt. A strong wind current had carried out the ashes from an erupting volcano and dumped them directly on us.

Several days later when the four o'clock watch reported on duty, Black Jack complained "the damned old boiler had been spurting steam all night, though they shovelled as hard as they could." We were having engine problems and real trouble came before the next dawn.

The crash threw everyone to the deck. Off shore of a high-cliffed island we hit a reef, and the seas were running half way up those cliffs. An engineer was stationed with the firemen to keep them on the job. The water surged in until it was knee deep and the steam boiled out. All hands were ordered on deck. I'll never forget the crunching sounds that little ship made on that reef while her hull opened up further and further, until she turned over on her side. She held on the rocks. A lyle gun was fired. It propelled a line or rope between ship and shore and a swimmer in the fairly calm water followed it to shore where he tied it securely. A hawser, two inches in length, was attached, to which the bosun's chair was rigged and used to carry the crew and passengers ashore.

We never had a fire or life drill and only a few had life belts. We had a raft but no way to get it into the water. When the order came to abandon ship, the only lifeboat aboard was loaded with the passengers and part of the crew. It was lowered over the side, but a giant wave smashed it against the ship and it was

103

hauled back. They thought the boat could be launched on the other side. Had they attempted it they might have gone to their certain deaths, but the first mate ordered them back at pistol point. Instead, they were transported ashore, one at a time, in the bosun's chair on the ropes.

Sparks, the wireless operator, repaired his damaged instruments in time to send out SOS signals and received word that help was coming. A couple of fishing vessels eventually hove into view and, anchoring outside the reef, sent in lifeboats and picked up those who had been sent ashore in the bosun's chair.

Except for a skeleton crew chosen to remain aboard and help a rescuer tow the *Altoona* off the reef, the rest of us were taken off the ship. God rest her good old bones if the *Altoona* is in Davy Jones' Locker. She was a good ship.

We heard later that we had been off course due to volcanic eruption disturbing the magnetic force in the ship's compass.

HOME

As a seaman I made many trips in the Alaskan vicinity, but I tired of being a drifter after three years. I returned home in 1910 to join my brother in the pie business and eventually went into the restaurant line. The latter was probably because food had been a main concern of mine throughout my adventurous years.

Thus began my business career which ultimately led me to have interest in many different corporations, ranging in nature from oil, uranium to art.

I also came back to Denver to claim the blue-eyed blonde I remembered from early boyhood. Her name was Laurena Hodges and her parents had rented my family's beautiful home in West Denver after the death of my parents. At the time, my brother had been operating a dairy farm out in Arvada, and I peddled milk at five cents a quart. I was a shy, barefoot boy who left a gallon of milk a day at the Hodges' back door and waited for Laurena to come out with the empty milk bottles for refill. She would smile and I'd gaze at her in admiration.

I had thought of her in San Francisco and during the time I was with the Indians, so upon my return, my first quest was to find her. She was then seventeen and I had reached the age of twenty. On the twentieth of May, 1962, Laurena and I returned from a world tour in celebration of our golden wedding anniversary.

ADAM KETCHTOOYACK

The first missionaries to the village of Kake were run off by the natives. In time they came to stay and the Kakes gradually succumbed to the religion of the Salvation Army.

My father, Ketchtooyack, was one of these converts, and he became a devout Christian — in his own way. It was difficult for me to interpret the Bible for him, and, although he could not understand most of it, he was sincere in his efforts to learn.

His religion and time healed my Indian father's hurt at my running away. In 1915, he sent me a totem pole of myself, about two feet in length, that he had carved out of a single piece of wood. Topping it was the raised head of a bear symbolizing the raven clan of which I am a member. The figure is holding a bucket for bear grease and a knife. Inscribed were these words: "His name is Kawoo Klee Ka, Kake, Alaska, 1915." Kawoo was my Indian first name; Klee means "is now" and Ka means "man." "Kawoo (Gano) is now a man." With the carving was a short letter that someone had written for him:

> "My dear son,
> I send you this totem pole because I love you and wish you could be at home with us. Your mother, she wants you too.
>
> > Your father,
> > Adam Ketchtooyack"

In 1916 another letter came from him which reads in part:

> "My dear son,
> We miss you so much but are happy that you are

doing well in your business. We wish you would look for some boy to send us. If you send a boy it is your sister, if you send a girl it is your brother. God bless you. I am still in Salvation Army.

Your father,
Adam Ketchtooyack"

And this letter:

"My dear son,
I am sending you moccasins, buckskin moccasins for you and your wife and wish you would come and see me. Your mother is all well, no sick. Love.

Your father,
Adam Ketchtooyack"

For his birthday one year, I sent my Indian father the brightest bathrobe I could find. He loved bright colors. A month or two later, I received a note, thanking me for the "coat" which he said was keeping him extra warm while he made the circuit of his trap lines!

During a Rotary convention in Denver, 1932, I drove an Episcopal Vicar and his party to the mountains. They were visiting from Alaska. After the automobile trip, I invited them to my home for dinner and talked about the Kake Indians. The Vicar responded that he knew quite a few of my friends. He also said he had heard about the white man who had brought food to the Indians at the Seattle Exposition. He promised to take a message to my father.

Shortly after this visit with the missionary, I received a letter from Uncle Joe Cojete, written for him by an interpreter. My father was dead. The village of Kake had been burned to the ground and gradually rebuilt. The totem poles so traditional were extinguished about 1913 for the sake of appearances and sanitary reasons.* He wrote that my father had held a prominent part in the early progress of the village, working toward a new form of modern government and in the annals of history is recognized as a worthy citizen of Kake. Uncle Joe, brother to Adam, also asked me to please return for a visit.

The most amazing turn of events concerning the village of Kake, however, happened in 1960. An article appeared in the *Denver Post* about an Alaskan Indian who had just completed a banking course at the Central Bank and Trust Company of Denver. It stated that his name was Roy Peratrovich and that he was a full-blooded Tlingit Indian, from Kake, Alaska.

After immediate inquiry, I called him and began to speak the Tlingit dialect over the telephone to his wife. To hear their native tongue spoken so far from home was quite a pleasant shock. They were both well-spoken and educated. He, of course, knew many of my people and said, by tribal adoption, he was a relative of mine. He greeted me with great enthusiasm; he had known about the legendary Kawoo all his life and now the opportunity to meet with him had finally come. Roy is now the area tribal operations officer for Alaska.

When I had returned to Denver, my brother Clive received a letter from the parents of Harry Cohn. They were wealthy San Francisco optical people who had been friends with Clive before the earthquake devastated the city. They had traced Clive to Denver to learn if he knew whether their darling son was alive or dead. We could not disclose Harry's fate with the evil spirit of Cushtaka. Instead we informed them that we knew nothing of his whereabouts or about his being shanghaied. We thought perhaps they would rather live in hope of seeing him again. Whether we were right or wrong in making this decision, will be a question always in our minds.

---

*For more up-to-date information about totem poles in the Alaskan culture, read *Much About Totems*, a booklet copyright 1962 by Pacific Northern Airlines.

KAWOO RETURNS

I was the prodigal son, and when I returned, the *Petersburg Press* newpaper reported that I had created the biggest event Kake had ever seen. I had traveled around the world and then to the South Seas, to Australia and Asia, when I desired to retrace my steps and go back to the place of boyhood experiences at Kake, Alaska.

In late April of 1964, my wife, Laurena, and I departed by plane for Juneau. Roy Peratrovich met us at the airport. We were saddened to learn of the death of his charming wife. Roy had registered us in at the famous Baranoff Hotel where press conferences, radio and television appearances were awaiting us. Two chapters of the Beta Sigma Phi Sorority entertained Laurena with all the welcome of their sisterhood in Alaska. She is an International Honorary member of this immense international organization and their official parliamentarian.

The graciousness and friendship extended us in Juneau, by Roy and others was an inspirational foretaste of the kindness in store for us during our entire Alaskan visit. We have joined the thousands of visitors to Alaska who assert that our forty-ninth state surpasses others in courtesy and friendliness as well as promise of great productive development.

From Juneau we flew to Kake in a small seaplane which looked somewhat forbidding after the jets that had carried us on most of our travels. It was raining and snowing intermittently and we saw little scenery until we were almost to Kake, where we viewed the small settlement.

We were surprised and delighted at the dock landing to find most of the people of Kake on hand to greet us. We toured the village, four miles of road, which was utilized by only eight automobiles. We met Auntie Jo, so named because she mothers most of the young people as well as the elders. Her culinary ability is not surpassed anywhere. The Mayor, Mitchell Martin, Auntie Jo's brother-in-law, represents all that one could desire in our First Americans. He is highly respected by all.

Most of the arrangements for our welcome were under the expert guidance of the postmaster and owner of the local movie house, Thomas Jackson, Sr. We visited the schools and met with the teachers who are also of Tlingit origin. These people are proud of their heritage and this pride is manifested in their determination to excell in all branches of education.

After walking the full path of the town, we visited with the many new friends, and I found myself conversing with members of the older generation in Tlingit, almost as well as though more than fifty years had not elapsed.

In the evening we were escorted to the Alaskan Native Brotherhood assembly hall. The modern hall had been built through the united efforts of all the people of Kake. Postmaster Jackson presided as master of ceremonies over a gathering of the three hundred townspeople for the welcoming potlatch supper.

Several speeches were given, some in English, and some in Tlingit — which I presume was for my benefit. An invocation was beautifully sung by the local fifty voice acapella choir. We were seated with the community leaders in the center of this huge room, which is normally used for all the indoor athletic activities. The only two white men of Kake, and their wives, were not present, but we met them during our stay. The mayor recalled that only six people were alive today who knew Kawoo as the "little white Indian boy" and all the rest of the villagers knew him through legends.

110

There were more welcoming speeches and Laurena was presented gifts from the Alaska Native Sisterhood. A carved totem of the Killer Whale with its history was presented to us both by David Stuteen. He was one of the men who knew me when I was adopted into the tribe and given the name of Kawoo. Laurena was given an Indian name of Klah Khoo, meaning "in the berries." She was presented with a hand-made tablecloth of native design on which there was her newly adopted tribal insignia of the eagle.

I have developed sleight-of-hand through the years and am proud to label myself a prestidigitator. When called upon to perform, I do so gladly. However, here at Kake, I insisted that my friends and "relatives" give me their assurance that they would not accuse me of witchery. Promises were amusedly given, but Laurena said she heard murmurs of "Custaka" when I accomplished incomprehensible sleight-of-hand tricks.

Following the potlatch we showed pictures of our world travels in the movie house. The audience was interested in all the films and enjoyed most viewing the native costumes of other countries.

We spent the next day visiting again and reminiscing about my sojourn in Kake so long ago. Amid all the chuckling, I learned that I was a "wild boy" when they found me living primitively on one of the Keku islands. I had long, light, sun bleached hair. Karl Williams, who boasts eighty-one years of living, proudly declared that he was "Kawoo's barber." He had started to cut my hair with a hunting knife when the woman who later became my Indian "Eclaw" protested his approach. She gave Karl an old pair of shears, but he could not make them work, probably because he was left-handed, and he continued to use the knife. Karl said: "When I had finished cutting, I was as scared as Kawoo, for he looked like he might be the Custaka." I remember being equally frightened of the knife being thrust at me so wildly.

111

Most of the people of Kake are now devout Christians, and the Salvation Army and the Presbyterian faith are the accepted creeds. On Wednesday, my wife and I were guests of Lieutenant and Mrs. Charles DeWitt of the Salvation Army in their attractive chapel. We were officially installed into the Alaska Native Brotherhood and Sisterhood organizations, and, again, precious gifts were presented to us by Mrs. DeWitt and the chairman of the Presbyterian association. This was followed by a songfest in which Laurena participated by singing the Evening Prayer.

I especially wished to see again the dances which at first had frightened me in those early days but later intrigued me. I persuaded Bob Thomas to assemble the dancers once more, though they had not attempted such a program in many years. On Thursday in the assembly hall, more than fifty costumed dancers performed while the drums boomed accompaniment. Songs in the Tlingit dialect told of the days of long ago.

During the ceremony, I, Kawoo, in full Indian regalia, was promptly recognized by song. I responded with the customary gift and in exchange received a kiss from the singer who had so honored me. Laurena was honored in like manner. This reenactment of this early culture, which is now almost nonexistent, is now preserved on movie film.

During all this, I was laughingly told that Kawoo had been considered to be a "bad boy" who violated the manners of conduct regarding respect for elders. To the Indians, bedtime was story telling time. The stories had no ending because they were intended to put the young to sleep. Each night the story was continued. I did not understand why these tales were not consistent with fact and constantly interrupted with questions. Apparently because I had been the privileged one of the tribe, I was not punished and was therefore unaware of the misdemeanor.

I did not intend to leave without seeing again the horror island where I had survived miraculously before being rescued by

112

the Indians. So I chartered a bush plane, piloted by capable Bill Stedman, and, with my friend Karl Williams, revisited my old hunting and fishing grounds including the sight of the old Russian saltry, all of which are now completely deserted, isolated islands.

Friday morning we made ready for departure with a feeling of happiness in the gift of new and old friendships. With regret, Kawoo Ketchtooyack and Kla Khoo bade farewell to the wonderful people who had extended to us such kindness and courtesy.

Since our arrival home, we have received mail that informs us that the legendary Kawoo is once again real to the Kakes, and that his reappearance will supply conversational material for another fifty-nine years.

I had returned to pay tribute to the Kake people to whom I am indebted for saving my life.. Though I have been in high places, and with dignitaries have supped, I never have received such warm hospitality filled with the glow of the Christian spirit, as when I revisited my adopted town of Kake.

Senter

Mr. and Mrs. Gano Everett Senter of Denver recently celebrated their 70th wedding anniversary with a reception.

They were married Aug. 29, 1911, in Denver, where Senter was employed by the Denver Sales Co., until his retirement in 1961.

Mrs. Senter, who is retired from the Emily Griffith Opportunity School, teaches painting in her home.

The Senters have two daughters, Laurena Evans of Littleton and Alice Maercklein of Englewood; four grandchildren and eight great-grandchildren.

Mr. and Mrs. Senter

1976

The Post
CONGRATULATES
Senter

Mr. and Mrs. Gano Everett Senter celebrated their 65th wedding anniversary Aug. 29. They were married in 1911 in Denver.

Senter has been a businessman and has authored a book about his early life.

Mrs. Senter, the former Laurena Hodges, has been active in community work and is a teacher of parliamentary procedure.

The couple has held open houses in December every year for the public to view their extensive collection of Christmas ornaments.

The Senters have two daughters, Laurena Evans and Alice Maereklein. There are four grandchildren and four great-grandchildren.

Mr. and Mrs. Senter

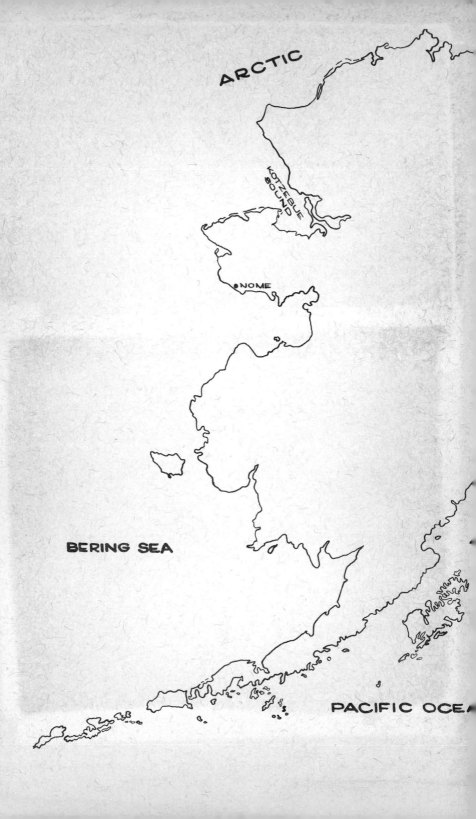